A
History of
Ideas

Published in 2023 by The School of Life
First published in the USA in 2023
930 High Road, London, N12 9RT

Copyright © The School of Life 2023

Designed and typeset by Marcia Mihotich
Printed in Latvia by Livonia Print

A proportion of this book has appeared online at
www.theschooloflife.com/articles

Every effort has been made to contact the
copyright holders of the material reproduced
in this book. If any have been inadvertently
overlooked, the publisher will be pleased to
make restitution at the earliest opportunity.

The School of Life publishes a range of books on
essential topics in psychological and emotional
life, including relationships, parenting,
friendship, careers and fulfilment. The aim is
always to help us to understand ourselves better
and thereby to grow calmer, less confused and
more purposeful. Discover our full range of
titles, including books for children, here:
www.theschooloflife.com/books

The School of Life also offers a
comprehensive therapy service, which
complements, and draws upon, our published
works: www.theschooloflife.com/therapy

ISBN 978-1-912891-96-2

10 9 8 7 6 5 4 3 2 1

A
History of
Ideas

The School of Life

I.
Historiography

Jacob de Wit, *Truth and Wisdom Assist
History in Writing*, 1754

It is – viewed from the perspective of our own age – a distinctly unusual painting. Sitting half-naked with her back to us, her hair beautifully braided, filling in a long scroll, is the allegorical figure of History. Assisting her on the left is the helmeted Greek goddess of wisdom, Athena; and above her resting on a cloud is the figure of Truth, naked – because she has nothing to hide – but covering certain parts – because she can never be fully known. At History's feet, three angelic children are helping out with background research. The title points us to the moral: *Truth and Wisdom Assist History in Writing.*

The painting was commissioned in the Netherlands in the mid-18th century for the entranceway to the private library of a keen amateur historian and wealthy Jewish-Dutch businessman, Isaac de Pinto, who lived in a house on Amsterdam's Nieuwe Herengracht. It conveys a strikingly grand impression of the significance of history, which probably has little to do with how we might remember the subject from school. Many of us may recall only a boring and disjointed ramble through items ranging from the Thirty Years War to the Viking invasions, or from Medieval crop rotation to the Treaty of Versailles.

The modern age may have made huge strides in how to write technically accurate history: we now know far better than our predecessors how to locate, archive and interpret original sources. But along the way, we seem to have lost a vivid sense of why we should bother with the past. How could the slew of information we have from previous ages be of use to us, outside of having to pass an exam? What, essentially, is the point of history?

The clue to the traditional answer, now largely forgotten but distinctly relevant to our times, is to be found in the Dutch painting in the helmeted figure of Athena. As the Classical goddess of wisdom would have reminded Isaac de Pinto on his way in and out of his library each day: the true point of history is to help to make us wise. Wise doesn't mean 'smart' or impressive to others. It means that through a judicious study of the past, we may learn how better to cope with life's vicissitudes; we may acquire greater calm and perspective in relation to opposition and reversals, crises and sorrows. We may understand ourselves more clearly. History – a topic that we might previously have associated with abstract and impersonal concerns (the foreign policy of Charlemagne, life at the court of the Inca emperor Atahualpa) – may offer us intimate assistance with how to deal with our tendency to panic, how to approach a troubled relationship or confront an unfair rumour about us at work.

However, to benefit from this rarer but more impactful kind of history – what we can call wise history – we may have to approach the raw material of the past differently from the way it is now mostly handled. We can keep our clothes on, we don't need angels or mythological figures, but we need to cut across history in unfamiliar and more philosophical ways. We can study the same books, but we need to make new selections from them: rather than a rendition of facts and events, we need to go in search of helpful ideas with a power to illuminate and console our psyches. We need to raid history with a very particular mission in mind: to learn how to live and die well. Athena would have understood, and svelte Truth approved.

George Rose, *Grammy Awards,*
Los Angeles, California, 1979

Squatting at the centre of our societies is an immensely powerful force that operates with two distinctive ideas: it tells us that *very new things are happening all the time* and, moreover, that *the new and the important are wholly synonymous*. That's why the media – or 'the news' as it tellingly calls itself – constantly and breathlessly barges into our lives, shouting about some event or other that, it insists, is radically different from anything else that has ever unfolded in the last 300,000 or so years of human existence and that we must drop everything to learn more about it right now.

However, when it is done properly, that is, with an eye on increasing our wisdom and bolstering our sense of peace, history directs us towards a very different, far more calming and far more useful notion: that, contrary to what we are being pestered into believing, most of what happens in the present is, in fact, only a repetition of something very similar that once happened in the past. The story of the ruler who lets power go to their head, of the government that forgets its responsibilities, of the young who are intolerant and self-righteous, of the beautiful person overcome by vanity ... these stories are as cyclical as the seasons and as enduring as the stars.

There are far fewer human types than there are people, far fewer principles than there are phenomena and far fewer ideas than there are commotions.

The American invasion of Iraq (2003) was a rerun of the Athenian invasion of Sicily (415–413 BCE). The mixture of naivety and pride of the last president of the Republic of South Vietnam, Nguyễn Văn Thiệu (1923–2001), was similar to that of the last Ming Emperor of China, Zhu Youjian (1611–1644). Our grandmother may in key ways be a double of Chaucer's (d. 1400) fictional Wife of Bath. The antics of a current celebrity resemble those of a 3rd-century Roman aristocrat. A complaint levelled against a government today was prefigured in a book by the German historian and social theorist, Max Weber, in 1914. The delusions of a contemporary political group were acutely captured in a pamphlet by Edmund Burke in 1789.

Wise history teaches us to look out for patterns; it directs us to laws of human nature, and principles of psychology that apply across time and space. With our minds well stocked with analogies, there will be so much less to surprise and shock us. We will know that we have seen this before – maybe in a provincial capital in China in 782 or on the coast of Central America around the time of the Spanish invasion. With history in mind, we can cease to be bewildered by shadows – and concentrate instead on the lights from which they originate.

Nicolas Poussin, *The Plague
of Ashdod*, 1630–1631

3.

At moments of particular despair and fear, history teaches us that we are – despite expectations to the contrary – no strangers to suffering; life may be awful now, but it was awful then. Problems have hounded us from the start. What seems difficult and unsurvivable today has occurred an immense number of times before, often in worse forms, and has been recovered from, once panic and a sense of persecution subside.

In early 1629, an appalling plague broke out in northern Italy. Corpses piled up in public squares. Whole families were wiped out in a matter of days. Doctors were helpless. The French artist Nicolas Poussin (1594–1665), then living in Rome, was shocked by reports of the suffering and chaos. But he also knew how to draw consolation from his knowledge of the past. In a painting that he composed in response, titled *The Plague of Ashdod*, Poussin depicted an outbreak that had ravaged the people of Israel in biblical times, not in order further to panic his viewers, but to reassure them that they were not alone in history – and would, with enormous pain, despite understandably bleak predictions, eventually recover.

Poussin was a keen historian and knew well enough what humanity had been through across the centuries. He knew that, in the 27th century BCE, the Nile had failed to flood for seven successive years and caused one of the first and largest famines in Egyptian history. He knew that, in 115 CE, an earthquake had hit the ancient city of Antioch, destroying three-quarters of its buildings and killing half of its 500,000 inhabitants. He knew that the first global bubonic pandemic had reached Constantinople in 541 and felled 50 million; that the 'Black Death' had arrived in Europe in 1347 and carried off 25 million; and that Hernán Cortés had landed on the shores of what is now Mexico in 1519, bringing with him in his saliva a smallpox virus that would, over the next hundred years, wipe out 90 percent of the native population of Central and South America.

Suffering cannot be directly removed by such knowledge, but fear and paranoia may be. When compared with our sunnier hopes of a few years back, our current predicament may be bleak indeed, but what has happened does not violate the ground rules of existence. We should be less impressed by lurid modern emphasis on the unparalleled nature of our catastrophes. Of course we are in trouble – but we always have been. History urges fortitude; we were never promised a clean sheet. Few of us ever escape without breakdown, abandonment, illness and failure; these are the almost inevitable burdens of being human, which we must anticipate and steel ourselves for. We should not rail nor tremble, whispers history, but simply expand the lens through which we look at the injuries that befall us. We have been here before; and this too will – however imperfectly, and with much agony – one day pass.

Sigmund Freud's desk in his study
at 20 Maresfield Gardens, Hampstead,
London

Sigmund Freud (1856–1939) may have been firmly on the side of modernity and an ardent advocate of technological and scientific breakthroughs. However, he was also steeped in the past and rarely looked at any modern phenomenon without trying to draw a connection from it to a historical event or idea.

It was evidence of his way of thinking that one-third of his large desk in his consulting room in Vienna was given over to historical figurines that he had collected over the years, made of marble, stone, bronze and wood – and drawn from diverse eras and cultures. There were examples from Pharaonic Egypt, Classical Greece and Rome, Confucian China and Pre-Columbian Mesoamerica. When Freud had to flee Austria at the advance of the Nazis, he carefully packed the figures away himself and rearranged them exactly as they had been in Vienna in his new home in Hampstead. They can be seen to this day in what is now the Freud Museum.

Freud's overwhelming concern in his work was to help us to make sense of our emotional drives and to explore the unfamiliar recesses of our characters. But he also appreciated that if this was the ultimate goal, then it could not be accomplished only or exclusively by reflecting on ourselves in isolation; it was crucial to align our experiences with the history of humanity. He proposed that many dynamics of our psyches are invisible to the explanatory mechanisms afforded to us by our own times and can only be adequately explored via the mentalities of other cultures and eras. A key to unlocking a part of ourselves might lie in ancient Sanskrit philosophy or a myth from the Babylonians. It was, for Freud, as if every age and civilisation was perfectly equipped to illuminate with special ingenuity some aspect or other of our own confused natures.

A person might – for example – be able to best grasp their feelings towards a parent by reflecting on a character from Greek tragic drama in the 5th century BCE. Eros, the Greek god of love, might help a spouse to make sense of their tangled sexuality in the bedrooms of modern Austria. Thanatos, son of the goddess of night, might deepen our grasp of our puzzling attraction to death. Listening to his patients ascribing blame to people from their childhoods, Freud's mind turned to Thoth, Egyptian god of wisdom. Often represented as a baboon (Freud had one on his desk), Thoth was in charge of a ceremony in which the hearts of all humans were to be weighed and their value decided upon at their death.

It was, for Freud, no disservice to the ages of history – no insult to Thoth, Thanatos, Eros or Oedipus – to be invited to explain and name the distempers and complexities of our minds. He appreciated that we can best come to know ourselves by thinking very hard and very personally about cultures that may lie extremely far from our own. History is a storehouse filled with exiled parts of ourselves.

Footprints of the Buddha
(Buddhapada), ancient kingdom
of Gandhara, Kushan Empire,
2nd century CE

In northern India, by the 1st century CE, it became common to depict the Buddha in stone not as a smiling statue (as would later become the norm) but as a set of large and squared-off footprints. These Buddhapada, as the sculptures were known, were fixed to the walls of temples and private shrines or embedded in pavements or parks.

The Buddha had been the wisest man who had ever lived. He had discovered how to achieve everlasting calm, understood how to become impervious to evil and indifferent to wealth, and learnt how to reconcile himself to mortality. It was, therefore, incumbent on any human to try to follow in his footsteps – each of which was imprinted in sculpture with two lotus flowers, symbolising purity, and a three-tipped Triratna, evoking the Threefold Way. On either side of these noble footsteps, yakshis, Indian sacred spirits, bowed in veneration.

The tradition of the Buddhapada is likely to feel usefully odd to us. We are constantly encouraged to make our own way through the world. There should be no walking in anyone else's footsteps, however grand these might be. We assume that we would lose a vital part of that all-too-precious commodity – our individuality – if we were to subscribe to ideas other than those that happen spontaneously to come into our minds.

Buddhapadas beg to differ. They imply that – so long as we find the right feet – we can only be enhanced by modelling our lives on those of well-chosen figures. The point is not to become more 'ourselves', in a random and wilful way, so much as to reach a state of wisdom and peace, which might well mean borrowing heavily from minds more nimble and perspicacious than our own, of which history can provide us with a wide-ranging library. Far from taking us away from our true selves, the thinking of others may be what offers us a path to our own latent potential.

As children, we perhaps all had the idea of putting our feet in our parents' enormous shoes and giggled at the unlikely strangeness of them, wondering if we would ever really one day grow into comparable giants. Because our parents may not, in retrospect, seem like ideal role models, the idea of walking in another's shoes can now feel doubtful. But, with the help of history, we may look beyond the figures of our early youth and scan past ages in search of other, more suitable candidates: Socrates or Montaigne, Donald Winnicott or Matsuo Bashō, Edward Hopper or Ella Fitzgerald. It shows a healthy degree of self-possession not to mind too much, at points, ceding to the ideas of thoughtful and visionary long-dead strangers. We aren't really alone, and we don't have to be without direction; we simply need to discover a set of footprints that will fit us.

'Kogetsudai' (moon viewing platform),
Temple of the Silver Pavilion, Kyoto,
c. 1490

In Medieval Japan, a group of thinkers emerged who felt that it might be of great benefit to people if they spent more time gazing up at the moon. They argued that careful contemplation of the moon can help to calm anxiety and restore perspective. To encourage the habit, they built special platforms – what they called *kogetsudai* – in gravel gardens around Kyoto and inaugurated a practice of regularly meeting on their summits on clear evenings to look at the sky, read poems and eat rice cakes. The practice proved so therapeutic that it spread rapidly around the country, and moon gazing became an integral part of the Japanese way of life for the next 300 years.

Like a lot of ideas that we find in history, *kogetsudai* can sound at once very strange and also, perhaps, intriguing. We might wonder: *Why don't we do something like this now? What could we use from here that could benefit our own times?* In certain cases, we might even ask: *What can we steal?* Such questions could sound heretical, but they suggest a hugely flattering notion of history: that it might be *useful* rather than merely academically important.

A lot is always missing from our societies. Marriages are difficult; loneliness is widespread; cities are ugly; manners and kindness have disappeared; rich people spend money in awful ways; the arts and fashion are disconnected from profound ideas; it's hard to hold on to sincere values … The temptation can be to give up. Yet we should dare to locate hope and inspiration in well-chosen pockets of the past.

Someone wanting to rethink what a marriage might be could – for example – learn much from the ideas of the Troubadour poets of 11th- and 12th-century Provence, who proposed that a good relationship should always place friendship far above sex and that psychological connection may be increased by delaying physical contact. Someone wanting to combat loneliness might learn from studying the way that the Epicurean philosophers of ancient Greece set up a network of communes combining fellowship with intellectual life. Those appalled by modern urban planning could derive useful lessons from the ambitions and practices of Venetian and Florentine architects of the early modern period. In the history of the courts of 17th-century Europe, there are fruitful ideas about how manners can be reformed and cruel impulses artfully softened. Renaissance Italy provides rich business people with a model of how money can best be spent in order to foster genius and beauty. Zen Buddhists can teach us how to anchor spiritual ideas in material practices (tea drinking, gravel raking, flower arranging …). The examples could go on.

A better future can be assembled by amalgamating a range of practices and solutions from the past. We don't have to recreate eras wholesale; we can borrow nimbly from their best moments. We don't, for example, have to set up actual religious monasteries or Epicurean communities to be inspired by a few things about them when designing our own communal spaces or schools of life; we don't have to become Buddhists to learn some good ideas about using architecture to mould our minds. We can steal what we need without having to descend into kitsch or slavish imitation.

The true lover of history is someone who dares to put the best ideas of the past to use in the urgent task of rendering the present a little kinder, more attractive and less frantic.

Fra Carnevale, *The Ideal City*,
c. 1480-1484

Friedrich Nietzsche (1844–1900) was one of the greatest historians and philosophers of all time. And in 1874, he published one of the best essays ever written about how to approach history. 'On the Uses and Disadvantages of History for Life' set out to define what the point of history should really be.

We need history, certainly, [wrote Nietzsche] but we need it for reasons different from those for which the idler in the garden of knowledge needs it, even though he may look nobly down on our rough and charmless needs and requirements. We need it for the sake of life and action ... History belongs above all to people of deeds and power, who crave models, teachers, comforters and cannot find them among their contemporaries. Their goal is happiness, perhaps not their own, but often that of a nation or of mankind as a whole.

Nietzsche was especially keen to show us how we might learn from the example of Renaissance Italy – especially its devotion to beauty, intelligence and wisdom – and wanted us to borrow heavily from certain of its lessons. He couldn't forget how few leaders of this movement there had been and that one rich banker, Lorenzo de' Medici, had pretty much single-handedly funded the greatest transformation ever effected in Western consciousness – and it only cost him 663,000 florins (about US$460 million today) to do so:

A person can learn from history that the greatness that once existed may be possible again; he goes his way with a more cheerful step, for the doubt that assailed him in weaker moments has now been banished ... Supposing someone believed that it would require no more than a hundred men educated and actively working in a new spirit to do away with the bogus form of culture which has just now become the fashion in Germany, how greatly it would strengthen him to realise that the culture of the Renaissance was raised on the shoulders of just such a band of a hundred men.

We currently treat the Renaissance with kid gloves. It sounds respectful, but the approach hints at underlying despair – for it implicitly suggests that we will never succeed as well again, and that we can only be preservers rather than originators of achievement. But this doesn't indicate real respect. The best homage we can pay the noblest ages of the past is to study them with an intent to emulate them – holding on to the thought that we could do as well, if not much better, going forward. That would be true fidelity to long-gone greatness.

Anonymous Venetian artist,
*Reception of a Venetian Embassy in
Damascus*, c. 1511

8.

We think ill of escapism. We tend to direct our admiration towards those who stick around and face their own times with courage.

Still, when everything has been said about the virtues of anchoring ourselves firmly to the present, there is also – at points – a case to be made for an opposing move: for the virtue of sometimes absenting ourselves from current circumstances and heading off in our minds to more distant, more bearable and more interesting ages, in which we can recover our poise and strengthen our powers.

We should, at moments, be allowed to admit to longing to be living in a different age, and not to have to think about all the things that people of our times are so strongly supposed to be obsessed by. We may not always want to worry as we're told to, or appreciate the famous person we're meant to admire, or be incensed by the political events that are meant to outrage us. We may want to take pride in not knowing the name of someone deemed to be the summit of bravery (or of idiocy), or of having no clue about a particular song or sporting event.

We might – instead – secretly want to accompany a set of what would now be called Venetian trade representatives on a mission to Syria in the 16th century, when the country was at a crossroads of East and West, to get better prices for yarns from Persia and cardamon from China. We might want to browse in Damascus' grand bazaar, then the greatest shopping arcade in the world, or go off to the royal baths, decorated in astonishing floral patterns of silver and azure tiles, adjoining the main mosque. Or we might simply want to stare in admiration at the exotic cypress and palm trees in the Emir's garden, vividly contrasted against the unusual pale blue of the Levantine skies.

There are, in the end, perhaps enough people fretting right now about the present moment. We have done our fair amount of it too – and will do so again, no doubt. For now, without telling anyone else, we might for a little while be allowed to evade our anxieties and our disappointments with a period of rest in one of history's many charming byways.

François Boucher, *Chinoiserie*,
c. 1750

As the more severe sort of scholars will tell us immediately, François Boucher (1703–1770) got it all wrong. Confucian sages didn't dress like that, and nor did their young mistresses. Pavilions didn't have exactly those roofs, or at least not in the southern part of China where this was meant to have taken place. And Chinese fishing rods certainly didn't bend so flexibly, being generally made of thicker and more stout bamboo poles.

Boucher's work can, therefore, at once be banished to a damning category of under-researched, historically inaccurate fantasy-based art, and from there take its place beside equally error-strewn depictions of ancient Roman baths and Native American encampments, ancient Egyptian feasts and Sumerian coronations.

The charge can't be wholly denied. Boucher had never been to China. He had fallen in love with the place from thousands of kilometres away, largely through books he had read by certain fanciful European explorers, Marco Polo among them, and original scrolls from the Ming and Qing dynasties that he had seen in the hands of Parisian aristocrats and that depicted mountains in the mist and elegant scenes from the court of Zhu Youyuan.

Arguably, Boucher did something even more important than get everything right about another culture. He found his way to certain things that deeply moved and interested him about it, and then put these to use in his own life. His version of China was, in terms of his development, as valid and as important as the fully detailed real thing might have been. It allowed him to achieve some distance from the oppressive French social system; its Confucianism counterbalanced the influence of the Bible; and its attitudes to sexuality and friendship allowed the painter to rethink his own, till then constricted, assumptions.

We are severely limiting what the past can do for us when we insist on placing the claims of accuracy far above those of inner nourishment. Fortunately for us and for him, François Boucher knew better than to let a crippling obsession with facts get in the way of wisdom.

Robert Adam, The Etruscan Room,
Osterley House, London, mid-1770s

10.

Though it's hard fully to admit this, when we get deeply interested in a period of history our true fantasy isn't just to read about it, it's sometimes to want to live there. That is, we don't simply want to learn about ancient Rome from Suetonius or Seneca, but we may aspire to be a Roman, to move about in a world which seems grander, more elegant, more sexually interesting and more intelligent than our own.

Such a wish might sound peculiar, but we should note that an entire tranche of the 18th-century British aristocracy more or less shared it for a hundred years or more. Inspired by the systematic excavations of Pompeii and Herculaneum and, in particular, the discovery of a series of exquisite wall paintings done up in what became known as the Etruscan style, wealthy Britons of the mid-18th century sought to redecorate their houses to look ever more like those of their predecessors in the ancient Roman empire.

Many of them gravitated towards employing the services of Robert Adam (1728–1792), the best-known architect of his generation, who developed a pared-down, neo-Classical style marked by a new fidelity to original Roman designs. The owners of grand houses like Syon House in Brentford, Kedleston Hall near Derby and Kenwood House in Hampstead ended up with interiors that resembled stage sets for ideal re-creations of Roman life.

We seldom begrudge children their wish to dress up as pirates or explorers; we understand that there are parts of them that need to be bolstered through engagement with alternative professions and civilisations. In that case, we shouldn't logically direct any particular mockery at adults when similar aspirations to expand their self-conceptions lead them to do up the dining room walls and chairs in a style that last prevailed on the Italian peninsula before the fall of the Roman empire.

There are as many, and perhaps more, of us who feel that we are living in ill-fitting times as in ill-fitting bodies. We should allow people a stigma-free opportunity to scrap their traditional décor and shift themselves imaginatively into an alternative era.

Thomas Rowlandson, *The Pedant*,
c. 1800

11.

It sounds odd, because we aren't used to thinking that you could have too much of a good thing like accuracy. It would be like saying that someone was too intelligent or too good a writer. But, like any virtue, a demand for precision can spill over into excess – as the remorseless late-18th-century English caricaturist Thomas Rowlandson (c. 1756–1827) well knew.

There are ways of handling historical material that forget why we might be doing it in the first place. The point isn't to pass an exam or impress a reviewer, to try to dazzle strangers with one's erudition or vaunt oneself before the memory of a withholding parent. The idea is simply to try to get better, kinder, calmer, wiser ... And in the pursuit of that goal, it really might not matter if we get one or two dates wrong or if we slightly misspell the name of the third to last emperor of the Inca dynasty (Huayna Capac).

It can take us a long time to leave school in our minds. Our bodies might not have set foot in such a place in three decades, and yet inside, we may still tremble before the imagined ire of a dour and critical teacher.

We have responsibilities far graver than we do to the Incas or the examination board. As Rowlandson knew, there should rightly be limits to our demands for erudition; we don't need to footnote everything or provide sources at every turn. We are at risk of forgetting who we are really working for. We may need at points to be consciously 'bad' historians in order to grow to be something more important still: wise humans.

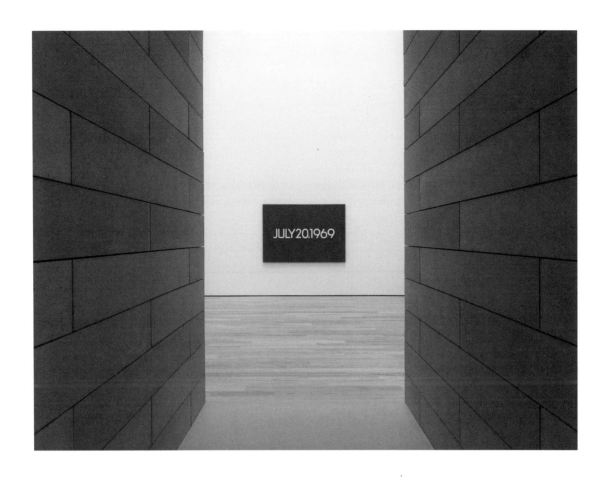

On Kawara, *Moon Landing* (detail),
1969, from 'Today' series (1966–2013)

If there is a generalisation to be made about the West's ideas of intelligence and profundity, it's that it tends to equate these qualities with length: the cleverer someone is, the more they are expected to write. A great number of the West's most revered books - *War and Peace, Middlemarch, In Search of Lost Time, The Decline and Fall of the Roman Empire, Don Quixote, Being and Time* - are, above all else, extremely long. The first true Western classic, Homer's *Iliad*, runs to over 700 pages in some editions.

The opposite is frequently the case in the East. There, length can be associated with muddled thinking, decadence and unwarranted elaboration, while the real effort and glamour is directed towards concision. It is no coincidence that the most lauded poem in Japanese culture, *Frog*, is three lines long:

```
The old pond;
A frog jumps in —
The sound of water.

Matsuo Bashō, 1686
```

If things are kept short, it's because of an underlying belief that the task of art and literature isn't to drip feed us ideas and sensations: it's to spark our own imaginations so that we can begin to be creative and thoughtful by ourselves. The work of art is essentially a tool - albeit a hugely accomplished one - for bringing out capacities that are already latent inside us. The ultimate determinant of quality in a work of art is its power to ignite our own minds.

This notion helps to explain the attitude to history of one of Japan's most acclaimed conceptual artists, On Kawara (1932-2014). Kawara proposed that we are hardly short of historical data; we're typically overwhelmed by all that we have read and seen in pictures of important events. What may be missing is an opportunity to meditate on what these events really mean without distraction. There is already a history book in our minds; we need the stillness and encouragement to explore it.

It was to this end that Kawara made a series of large black paintings that he provocatively called history paintings and that featured only the date of a range of global events. There was no need to say anything else about these particular events (outside of their titles), felt Kawara; they were intended only as a fertile springboard for our own thoughts.

For example, we already know rather a lot about NASA's moon landing of 1969; but what we've perhaps long been missing is the opportunity to let the event sink in as it should.

Kawara alerts us to a curious notion: that a really good historian isn't just someone who knows a lot about the past. It's someone who has given themselves the opportunity to feel what lies beneath a factual layer - a move that might require relatively few words and a surprising amount of blank space and time.

Pair of gold earrings with emeralds,
from Pompeii, Italy, 1st century CE

13.

We know almost nothing about the circumstances in which these Roman earrings came to be made, owned and abandoned. All that we can be sure of is that they were found near the skeletons of a family and a dog somewhere in the ruins of Pompeii in the mid-19th century – and that they would have lain there undisturbed since the fateful eruption of Mount Vesuvius in the late summer of 79 CE.

We can, nevertheless, imagine rather a lot simply by looking. We can imagine the care with which they were made by long-charred and decomposed Roman fingers. We can imagine their owner, a prosperous and elegant Roman woman, who could have had no inkling of her fate and the intentions of a nearby volcano that no one could remember ever having exploded. And we can – in a poignant but also uncomfortably intimate way – imagine how those earrings must have been affixed to two Roman earlobes, which – despite the distance that separates us – would have been so much like our own.

There is a lot that we can read about Pompeii, much of it fascinating: about who lived there, how the city was administered, how houses were decorated, and so on. In the end, the emotional impact of the destruction of this city and the deaths of so many of its inhabitants may best be felt when we allow ourselves to be quiet for a while, and let certain everyday objects speak to us across time, sparking personal reveries in which melancholy mingles with longing and grief.

We know, in theory, about so many things that have happened centuries ago; but we seldom allow ourselves to feel them as we should. The best tribute we might pay to the long-dead Roman lady and the civilisation of which she was a part might be to spend a minute – which can be a surprisingly long time – taking in the enormity of what these earrings have to tell us about the passage of centuries, about our own future, our death and, in a very quiet way, what we might as well term love.

Shen Yuan, *Up the River During
Qingming* (detail), Qing dynasty

One of the most famous works of classical Chinese art, often copied in later centuries, was a very lengthy and slender scroll, many metres long, depicting life along the Bian River as it makes its way to the capital, Bianjing (present-day Kaifeng) during the spring-time Qingming festival. People, then as now, travelled home to the tombs of their ancestors in order to sweep them clean and offer up ritual gifts and prayers.

Part of what makes the work astonishing is how much of 'life' it seems to contain, and how vividly it speaks to us across centuries. As we travel along the scroll, we are afforded an exceptionally detailed panorama of Chinese life; we see bucolic fields, villages, towns, palaces, temples, workshops, restaurants, markets and gambling dens. We meet meticulously drawn teachers, fortune tellers, innkeepers, scholars, government officials, hawkers, beggars and shoppers; some 4,000 people in all, along with thirty buildings, 200 trees and twenty-eight boats.

When we speak about the past, we're apt to sum up large slices of it in the briefest of terms, almost without noticing what we're doing; we make generalisations about 'life in the Qing dynasty . . .' or the 'rise' or 'fall' of a whole continent. Shen Yuan's scroll reminds us of the stupefying, summary-defying complexity of any century, year or day, let alone any city street, bridge or single human. Every one of those lives along the Bian River was as complicated and tempestuous as we know ours to be: inside every mind were as many thoughts, prejudices, whims, passions, loves and sorrows as roil through our own. The small expanse that every head occupies in space belies the number of universes that it contains at the level of feeling and imagination.

Most of us will leave no traces. What we call history is just the record of a minuscule number of events that, in the form of a monument or a book, an institution or a picture, somehow managed to evade the juggernaut of forgetting. The 13th-century Japanese master Eihei Dōgen (1200–1253) asserted in his collection of essays, the *Shōbōgenzō*, that a day consists of 6,400,099,180 moments (every moment being 1/74,000 of a second). We can quibble with the numbers, but the general point is clear: life is stupefyingly dense – and almost everything about it will disappear without leaving a mark.

Our impressions, our longings, our memories of childhood, the associations we have of the smell of the earth after rain, our nostalgia for our grandparents, our plans for the future, the nuances of our relationship to our in-laws . . . all of it will go, leaving a barren desert in which historians will airily decree the existence of phenomena like 'the rise of the bourgeoisie' or 'the growth of commerce'.

We cannot – and that is the point – know in any detail quite what has been lost across history; but we can at least, through our imaginations, while reflecting on the complexities of our own minds, derive a decent sense of how vast the domains of disappearance must be. We might think there is a lot of history to read about; the true and unavoidable tragedy is how much of life there once was, and how little of it made it through, as the river of time forged its way to the impassive eternal ocean.

Carbonised wooden cradle, found
in the House of Marcus Pilius
Primigenius Granianus, after
the eruption of Mount Vesuvius,
Herculaneum, Italy, 79 CE

15.

There are enormous gaps in the historical record. There are centuries where, in relation to understanding the lives of millions of people, we have nothing to go by – only a few pots or marks on a bone, one or two scraps of paper or a single ambiguous temple carving. What were they really thinking? What was in the minds of people on the Mongolian steppes in the 8th century CE? What happened in the kingdoms around the Niger River in the 5th century BCE? What was life like for the inhabitants of what is now Papua New Guinea during the long years of the reign of Elizabeth I of England?

Even where there is a degree of evidence, enormous gaps remain: it's impossible to know what 5th-century Britons really thought about male–female relationships or the cycle of the seasons. No ancient Mesoamerican remembered to tell eternity how they felt about dieting or insomnia. We have no clue how the Native tribes of the Pacific Northwest of America related to their siblings or dealt with missing a loved one.

Where there are gaps, standard historians have one overwhelming rule to impart to us: we must never, ever fill things in. It is definitively not our role to imagine what a Roman or an Inca, an Aborigine or a Ming dynasty Chinese thought. They either told us explicitly – or we should fall silent.

The rule is, at points, wise and full of good intentions, but it runs counter to an invaluable ability of which we are all capable by virtue of belonging to the human race: that of having a very good guess. We may not know a lot of things for certain – we may well think very differently from our forebears about gods or thunderstorms, chiefs or omens – but we have one advantage over a visiting alien. We are, in a host of areas, fundamentally identical to the people who lived on the shores of Akuna Bay or in the foothills of Mount Chopicalqui, the hamlets of the Iforas Massif or the streets of Ur. Sex, marriage, ageing, friendship, illness, pride, despair, terror … we can read of them in history books or, as plausibly and as usefully, in the stories of our own lives.

In a majority of situations where there is no formal evidence, the best way to find out what a Roman, an Aztec, a Macedonian or Goguryeo person would have thought is to ask ourselves what we think. If we want to know how a Carthaginian felt when, on a hot day, they ran into the refreshing ocean waves, or if we want to know how a Celt would have experienced a summer's evening or the smell of autumn, we don't need sources beyond ourselves.

Black-and-white photography has lent us an unfair impression of how the past might have looked, as if it might all have been like one of those sepia shots we know from the late 19th century. In truth, the light was as vivid and the colours as bright as they are today in 1843, in 970 or in 389 BCE. A tree, a meadow and a beach were identical at the time of the birth of the Prophet Muhammad and in the reign of Ramses II. Burping hasn't changed, nor has quarrelling with a friend, envying a rival, longing for bed, gulping water, hating a parent, tasting olives or touching a lover's skin. We can – in far more areas than is officially allowed – take a series of educated guesses.

Nothing survives to tell us exactly how the parents who lived in what is known to archaeologists as the House of Marcus Pilius Primigenius Granianus in Herculaneum felt about their recently born child: what that child was like to pick up, to put to sleep, to feed and to wash. Nor can we know what – if they themselves survived the eruption of Vesuvius – the parents thought about the death of their poor child, how long they mourned and what they remembered of him or her in the years after the tragedy.

But we don't need any evidence. We know already. We don't have to have a historian on hand, nor a long letter in Latin written on parchment. We just need to remember what it is like to be us – and the answer, and perhaps a tear, will follow automatically.

'A man showing his friends his
Cabinet of Curiosities.' Woodcut of
the Wunderkammer room, from Ferrante
Imperato, *Dell'historia naturale,
Libri XXVI*, Naples, 1599

Before there were museums, in many parts of Europe and beginning in the 16th century, wealthy educated people were in the habit of building themselves what were known as 'cabinets of curiosities' – rooms in their houses filled with unusual artefacts from history. A typical cabinet would be stocked to the brim with surprising and wondrous elements: there might be a Medieval shield, the skin of a crocodile, a suit of armour, a hand from a Roman statue, a sword from Morocco, a lock of hair from an Indian princess, a carpet from Persia, a fossilised fish, the tusk of a narwhal, the tooth of a saint, a picture of a rhinoceros or the pickled head of a zebra. After dinner with friends, the owner might take them up to the cabinet, open up the drawers and pull out the display cases – and together they would muse on the mesmerising strangeness of the past.

There are obvious advantages to museums (everyone can go, things are properly classified, fakes are weeded out), but the positive aspects of the sort of passionate and idiosyncratic relationships to history fostered by cabinets merit nostalgia. Too often, we now proceed through galleries without engaging our more individual faculties; our imaginations are on a tight leash. We don't look out for elements that excite us; we aren't primed to recognise our helpfully naive native enthusiasms. It can all be a little cold and a little dutiful.

It's implausible for most of us to begin our own cabinets at this point: suits of Medieval armour are hard to come by and pickled heads are not easy to maintain. An important essence of the old cabinet tradition, however, remains available. It is open to all of us to adopt the personally led, passion-driven approach to the past that animated the efforts of early collectors. We, too, can – in our minds – pull together the ideas, objects, anecdotes and thoughts that speak to us most vividly of bygone centuries and afford us elements of nourishment that our own era cannot provide.

It shouldn't be our aim to be comprehensive or entirely objective in our cabinet-building moves. We need only pick up bits of history for urgent, visceral and egoistic reasons: because they spark our dreams, they make us long, they calm us down, they cheer us up.

Museums of history are impressive – but they have priorities beyond seeking to console or counsel us. We should be sure to retain somewhere a small, private, imaginary cabinet of curiosities in which to arrange elements that can bolster our spirits, restore perspective and loosen us from the conformist mentality of our age.

II.
Prehistory

The concept of the universe: the
cosmic turtle featuring a snake
(cobra) and elephants. Unnamed artist
in *Les Indes Pittoresques*, 1850–1860

For a long time, we were – it can fairly be said – muddled about when, and how, it all began. Christians believed that the world had started in 4004 BCE; Islam maintained that the world had been 5,432 years old at the time of Muhammad's birth; Medieval Hindu cosmology was certain that things had kicked off 311.04 trillion years ago; while Aristotle insisted that the universe stood outside time altogether and had never had a beginning and would never have an end.

Explanations of the precise mechanics of the Earth's genesis were equally disparate. In Japanese cosmology, the world was said to have floated on a layer of oil and was as shapeless as a jellyfish, until two deities, Izanagi and his younger twin sister Izanami, emerged. They dipped a jewel-encrusted spear into the ocean and collected a drip at the end of it, which solidified and became an island called Onogoro. Brother and sister set up home on Onogoro and had a number of children, each of which became one of the islands that eventually made up the archipelago of Japan.

Chinese cosmology described the world as a giant egg that floated in a timeless void reverberating to two opposing forces, yin and yang. Eventually, the heavy molecules of the egg (yin) sank downwards and formed the Earth, while the lighter molecules (yang) rose up and formed the sky. At the same time, a giant man-like creature appeared called Pangu, whose task it was to ensure that Heaven and Earth stayed separate. To hold them apart, he grew ever taller (3 metres a day for 18,000 years) until he died and his body exploded into all the bits of the universe, including animals, other planets and clouds.

In Hindu cosmology, the world – pictured as a half-sphere – was vomited from the mouth of a serpent called Shesha, and was said to be held up by four (or in some accounts eight) sacred elephants standing on the back of a giant turtle called Chukwa, whose feet rested on the serpent's coils.

It took a long time for doubts about these stories to emerge, sparked by the varied discoveries of geology and palaeontology: a fossil 2 million years older than Adam and Eve would have been; a layer of rock and fossil ferns (*Glossopteris*) that was the same in South America as it was in western Africa, indicating that the continents must have been joined up in a single giant landmass 240 million years ago; the realisation that there must have been five mass extinctions, rather than one Noah and his Ark. The once-Christian art critic John Ruskin lamented in 1851 that his faith was being beaten to the thinness of gold leaf by the discoveries of geology: 'If only the geologists would leave me alone, I could do very well, but those dreadful hammers!'

We now know infinitely more about our beginnings than did our distant ancestors who dwelt a lot nearer to it. One of the great intellectual achievements of modernity has been the accurate delineation of our prehistory. We are used to thinking that the facts of science will always sound a great deal less fanciful than the myths of religion. When it comes to the origins of the world, though, the scientific narrative outstrips by many magnitudes the most phantasmagoric and implausible notions of our faithful forebears. Given what actually happened, the tale of the regurgitated turtle starts to sound like the sober one. Were an inspired guru to have put forward the account of the universe's beginnings that we now know, they would not have found a single believer among even the most credulous. By far the weirdest creation story ever told happens, remarkably, also to be the true one.

Explosion of the supernova SN2018gv,
located c. 70 million light-years
away from Earth, in the spiral galaxy
NGC 2525. It is unleashing a surge of
energy 5 billion times more intense
than that of our sun - as captured by
the Hubble Telescope.

2.

Once upon a time, 13.8 billion years ago, our immense universe was so tiny that it couldn't have been seen by even the strongest microscope. Everything that now exists – the atoms in one's fingers, the rings of Saturn, the ice on Jupiter's moon Europa – were crammed together into an infinitesimal point. But the energy therein was so intolerable that, in 10^{-32} of a second, the universe burst apart in an explosion whose waves of energy continue to expand outwards to this day at a rate of 67.4 kilometres per second per megaparsec. In an instant, the universe went from being smaller than an electron to having a diameter of 93 billion light-years across. At first, it contained only pure energy, which then formed into particles that rearranged themselves through gravity into the lighter elements hydrogen, helium and lithium, which combined to give birth to a trillion galaxies and a quadrillion stars.

Somewhere in the fourth galactic quadrant of this universe, in what we call the Local Cluster, a galaxy took shape called the Milky Way, which enclosed 100,000 million stars within a 200,000-light-year diameter. When, after a few billion years, some of these early stars got old, they became smaller and heavier, the pressure built up inside them and eventually some of them exploded into supernovas, which shot out immense clouds of dust and gas and tiny particles of iron and copper. Some 4.6 billion years ago, one of these clouds ended up travelling round a star 25,000 light-years from the galaxy's core; every so often two specks in the cloud would collide and stick together (a bit like pieces of fluff do) and this kept happening for millions of years until eventually practically all the dust had joined together to make eight planets, one of which – the third along from the sun – we now call Earth.

In the first billion years of this orbiting rock, the Earth was lifeless and very hot, 1,600°C on average. Meteorites kept smashing into it, bringing ice and minerals with them, which created seas and eventually an atmosphere. Then, around 3.5 billion years ago, most likely some-where deep in the quiet ocean in the vicinity of a hydrothermal vent, a special combination of carbon, hydrogen, nitrogen, oxygen, phosphorus and sulphur came together to create the self-replicating cellular phenomenon we call life. Our story had begun.

What can be summed up in a few paragraphs took thousands of scientists – true historians – 150 years to piece together. Rather than daydreaming about how it might all have started, they dared to go and find out. They were selfless and adult enough to resist the pull of fantasy and projection – and bound themselves to a professional code that immediately forced them to give up on theories that could not be substantiated before their colleagues (rather than encouraging them to burn these heretics at the stake). The story of creation is wondrous enough; the intellectual discipline and steadiness of mind behind its discovery is yet more so.

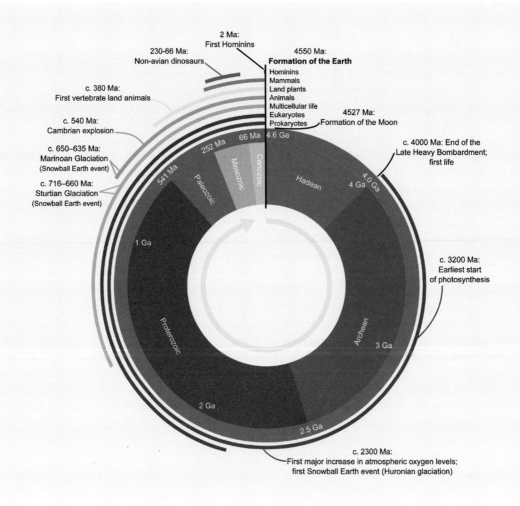

2 Ma:
First Hominins

230-66 Ma:
Non-avian dinosaurs

c. 380 Ma:
First vertebrate land animals

c. 540 Ma:
Cambrian explosion

c. 650–635 Ma:
Marinoan Glaciation
(Snowball Earth event)

c. 716–660 Ma:
Sturtian Glaciation
(Snowball Earth event)

4550 Ma:
Formation of the Earth

Hominins
Mammals
Land plants
Animals
Multicellular life
Eukaryotes
Prokaryotes

4527 Ma:
Formation of the Moon

c. 4000 Ma: End of the
Late Heavy Bombardment;
first life

c. 3200 Ma:
Earliest start
of photosynthesis

c. 2300 Ma:
First major increase in atmospheric oxygen levels;
first Snowball Earth event (Huronian glaciation)

252 Ma
66 Ma
4.6 Ga
541 Ma
Paleozoic
Mesozoic
Cenozoic
Hadean
4.0 Ga
4 Ga
1 Ga
Proterozoic
Archean
3 Ga
2 Ga
2.5 Ga

Geological clock: the history
of the Earth

If we were looking for a symbol for a new secular religion that could spread love, calm and goodwill throughout our fractious societies, it might be hard to find anything quite as effective as this: a geological clock that, across a diameter not much larger than that of an orange, shows – with supreme concision and deceptive simplicity – all the major events that have unfolded in the history of the planet since the day of its creation.

We would need to put up copies of such a geological clock everywhere that people might be in danger of losing perspective and of falling prey to rage and bitterness – in railway stations, company boardrooms, the consulting rooms of marriage therapists, family kitchens and holiday resorts. We could be confident that its chronology would, at speed, render us something far more valuable than punctual: serene and ego-less.

We could drown our painful sense of self-importance and our repeated frustrations with other humans in a renewed awareness of our blessed nothingness in the totality of the cosmos. We could nullify our sorrows in the aeons of Hadean and Archean time; we could dissolve our anger in the record of the billions of years of the Proterozoic age, in which nothing much stirred beyond the quiet pulses of armies of minuscule eukaryotes. We could take curious comfort in the thought that 99 percent of all life forms that have ever existed are now extinct.

Rather than attempt to meditate in a Tibetan way, we might commit certain key dates to memory and repeat the following as though it were a mantra:

13.8 bya:*	Creation: the Big Bang
4.6 bya:	Birth of our sun and solar system
3.8 bya:	Earliest life on Earth
1.8 bya:	The first eukaryote
600 mya:*	The first large organisms
535 mya:	The first fish
485 mya:	The first vertebrates
250 mya:	The first mass extinction
225 mya:	The first dinosaur
155 mya:	The first bird
66 mya:	Asteroid strike: no more dinosaurs
55 mya:	The first whales, horses, rabbits, elephants
30 mya:	The first cats
7 mya:	Human lineage splits from chimp lineage
2 mya:	*Homo erectus* walks
200,000 ya:*	*Homo sapiens*

And, most consolingly of all:

4.5 byfn:*	The sun will die

* Billions of years ago (bya), Millions of years ago (mya), years ago (ya), Billion years from now (byfn)

We might look at such a list three or four times a day; it might be set to music or turned into an opera. Our egocentricity would be challenged, but we would be rewarded with an attitude of continuous acceptance and grateful wonder. Scientific researchers have been unnecessarily humble: they haven't just explained where we've come from. They have offered us unparalleled tools with which to calm and rebalance ourselves.

Bornean orangutan (*Pongo pygmaeus*)
and young, Borneo

4

For most of our time on the planet, it has felt very important – and very comforting – to be able to deny that there might be any sort of link between them and us. The wall separating humans from animals has been kept very thick indeed in our imaginations.

There have been two strands to this denial. The first has involved stressing how little *they* have in common with *us*: they don't have language, they don't use tools, they don't build homes and they don't have feelings. And therefore, we should have little compunction about deforesting their habitats and parboiling them for dinner. Modern science, however, tells us a different story. It turns out that chimps use blades of grass to get termites out of their nests, that whales speak in a language of complex clicks, that the New Caledonian crow makes hooks to get hold of insects, that magpies perform funeral rites for their relatives and that African elephants talk to each other in a sequence of low hums audible up to 250 kilometres away. We might, in fairness, have to rethink what we put on our plate.

There is another, psychologically more pertinent, denial at work: the insistence that we have very little in common with *them*. Nature may compel animals to do all sorts of odd things: swim upstream in September, urinate to mark territory, put up feathers to attract a mate. Yet we're free to do whatever we like: go to nightclubs, buy sports cars, shop for new clothes and fret about giving a presentation about tax rates at the office.

Except, of course, that beneath a veneer of so-called free will, most of what we do is entirely synonymous with, and an elaboration upon, animal compulsions, as befits a creature that shares 98 percent of their DNA with a gorilla. We are unable to worry any less about our careers than would a deer about its antlers or a mandrill about its facial colourations. We sweetly forget the connections between our pride in our new apartment and the tail feathers of the sage grouse, or between our investment in a costly watch and the dance of the bird of paradise. We jostle at the office like versions of Eringer cattle. We are no less herd animals than musk oxen or wildebeest – and our minds are as prey to being imprinted upon by our early caregivers as newly hatched Canada geese.

All the same, we typically fail to detect the real source of our motivations. We claim to want kids because we find them 'sweet' – without squaring up to the awesome force within us that ensures we will find them so, whatever the true (much more debatable) evidence of what they are like. We speak of 'not fancying' one prospective partner while feeling charmed by another, and – naively – put the difference down to 'shared interests'. We repeatedly flatter ourselves into believing that we are choosing rather than obeying.

None of this should humiliate us, but rather free us to acknowledge the compulsive aspects to our choices and our concerns for status, fashion, beauty, money, gossip and fame. It's only been a very brief 7 million years since we shared a common ancestor with a chimpanzee; the bones in our hands are like-for-like identical to those in a horse's front legs, a bat's wings and a dolphin's fin. To sense afresh the connections between ourselves and animals shouldn't only lead us to be nicer to them; it should simultaneously inspire us to be nicer to ourselves; that is, more generous towards, and amused by, the many peculiar and irrepressible antics to which our animal nature continually subjects us.

A fennec fox (*Vulpes zerda*)

5

It's hard to think of an animal better adapted to the strange and difficult place it has to live than the fennec fox. In its native Saharan and Sinai deserts, the fennec has to cope with 40°C daytime temperatures, a near-complete lack of water, boiling sand, sparse food supplies and predatory vultures and jackals. Yet to each of these many challenges, it has arrived at ingenious solutions. Its vast ears, up to 15 centimetres long, help to dissipate heat and detect the slightest movement of lizards and geckos; it can allow its body temperature to rise to 40.9°C before it begins to sweat; it pants at a record-breaking 690 breaths a minute; it has specially adapted kidneys that produce hyperosmotic urine; and its fur covers its feet to give them traction and stop them burning as it runs across the hot sand.

To look at a fennec is to see evidence of 8 million years of evolution in relation to the rigours of one very specific habitat. We humans don't need to be jealous. We, too, were entirely well adapted to our original habitats: we acquired intensely fearful reactions that would alert us to predators, lusts that would help us find fertile mates, appetites for sugar that would help us maintain body weight and minds favouring snap judgements to evade snakes and sabre-toothed cats. We also had perfect spines for being on our feet all day.

There is, however, a major difference between us and the fennec fox. We no longer live in the environments to which we were originally adapted. Spines evolved to walk for kilometres across the savannah now slouch on office chairs; eyes honed to detect wild berries now focus in on another slice of polenta cake.

There have – it is true – been a few changes in our DNA over the last 60,000 years. Humans living in the Arctic have evolved to carry thicker layers of fat on their faces to reduce the risk of frostbite. Rice- and wheat-cultivating populations have gained an ability better to digest starch, thanks to the salival enzyme amylase. Around 6,000 years ago, a genetic mutation tweaked levels of melanin in northern populations and gave some of them blue eyes.

But no animal on Earth whose original habitat has altered as radically as ours has survived – while evolving as little as we have. We are doing well enough, but we should be forgiving when aspects of our historically evolved constitutions interact awkwardly with distinctive features of modernity. We are, at points, like a fennec fox forced to live in Hampshire, an African elephant trying to make its way in Baden Wurttemberg or a tropical rock lobster setting up home in the icy waters off Antarctica.

Genetic evolution moves a lot less quickly than does human history; many aspects of our minds and bodies are, therefore, relics. It should be no wonder that we often eat too much, watch porn all day, develop back ache, tremble at the thought of sharks and get statistics entirely wrong. It isn't narrowly our fault; a lot of who we are and of what we want just made a lot more sense in a world that no longer exists.

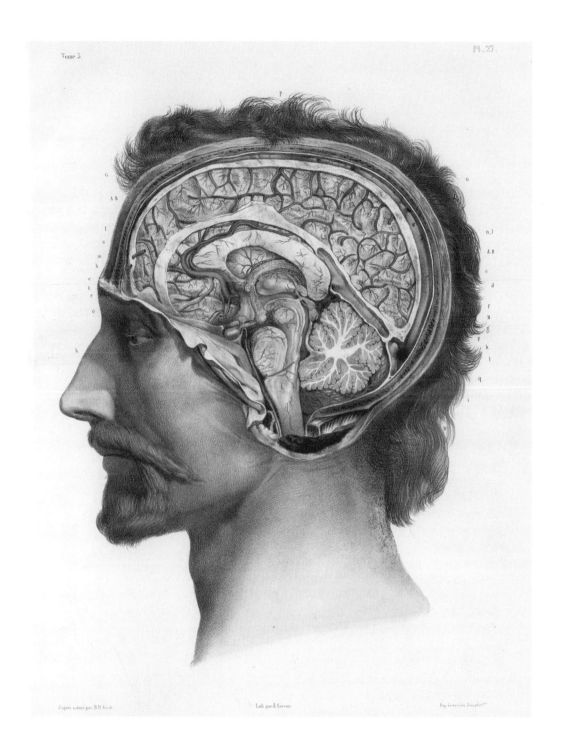

Median section of the brain.
Lithograph by A. Leroux, after a
drawing by N. H. Jacob. From the
third volume of *Traité complet de
l'anatomie de l'homme* by Jean Marc
Bourgery, 1866–1867

6

Most of humanity's problems can be traced back to the architecture of our brains. This brain is – above all else – a historically structured organ. We can't, and won't for a while, know its entire story, but we already understand enough to be certain that different faculties came into being at different points. We know that some parts (the amygdala) are 'older' – more primitive, more instinctive, more akin to what can be found in reptiles and birds – and that other bits (the cerebral cortex) are more 'recent' – more complicated, more patient and more focused on higher-order reflection and analysis.

We don't – minute by minute – have any instinctive sense of navigating with minds assembled out of components of widely varied degrees of sophistication. Consciousness appears unitary and seamless. We aren't able easily to notice that a particular response may be coming from a part of the mind that might owe a lot to a canine ancestor on an adjoining branch of the evolutionary tree. Nor can we accurately spot when a desire that would have made wholehearted sense on a grassy plain threatens to derail a life largely spent in business parks and high rises.

In his *The Descent of Man* of 1871, Charles Darwin reflected with melancholy on the way that 'man with all his noble qualities, with his god-like intellect which has penetrated into the movements and constitution of the solar system, with all these exalted powers, still bears in his bodily frame the indelible stamp of his lowly origin'.

Darwin was lamenting that even the most apparently civilised humans are only ever a short step away from aggression, panic, prejudice and viciousness. It is our damned 'lowly origins' that make it so hard for us to be reflective about our motives and desires. Introspection was evidently no early evolutionary priority; we survived by brute instinct and still prefer to navigate by it even in situations where all the benefit would lie in taking an issue apart through patient logic. Racked by anxieties, we cannot accurately assess what truly threatens us. Deep inland, far in the north, we're still predominantly scared of sharks and venomous snakes – while failing to fear what really threatens us: our haste, our naivety, our sentimentality and sloth.

At the same time, we reason wildly because of how heavily marked we are by certain of our early experiences. We may completely lose confidence in ourselves because one unfortunate figure humiliated us unbearably in childhood. We start to be suspicious of all men or all women because one particular example once made us suffer more than we could tolerate.

In love, we seek out people who resemble our early caregivers, even when this runs counter to our best interests. We continue to marry versions of our mothers and fathers, even and especially when they once made things hellish for us. We seem to far prefer what feels familiar to what is good for us.

We misjudge opposition; we grew up in small groups of a hundred or so where the opinions of a few people mattered a lot. Now we live among millions, but still take one or two vicious comments as verdicts that pose an unparalleled danger.

Our instincts insist on things far beyond what would be necessary for our development. We might need to make a few children; we think of sex at every turn. We need to ensure we consume enough calories to survive the day; we end up obese.

There is no solution to the problems posed for us by our historically flawed brains, beyond one essential move: knowing that we are demented, knowing that our brains are likely to be throwing out faulty readings at every turn, knowing how unreasonable we are. The only wisdom available to us is that founded on a vigilant awareness of our inherent tendencies to folly – and of the ineradicable traces of our intellectual kinship with some very excitable and very agitated early primate cousins.

Garry Winogrand, *New York*, 1961

7

One question that deserves to bother us throughout a trip to the zoo is: why isn't it *them* visiting *us*? Given how fragile, small and defenceless we are relative to other animals, how did we end up as the apex predator? Why don't families of mighty rhinos come to see us in our enclosures on the weekend, given their far greater strength, resistance to disease and ability to clear their way through forests? Not even a consideration of brain size resolves the conundrum. Sperm whales have vast brains: 8 kilograms next to our 1.3 kilogram ones; those of elephants are 5 kilograms; those of bottlenose dolphins, 1.7 kilograms. Why, then, are we in charge of the zoo?

The answer to what is one of the major riddles of history lies in something inside our brain structure that can't as yet be physically identified, but which we know by inference must exist, while remaining absent in everything else that has ever drawn breath and reproduced.

For most of our time on Earth, *Homo sapiens* wasn't appreciably different from any of its adjacent hominin relatives. For 200,000 years, we did our best with basic tools, we communicated a few simple things to one another with basic commands, we struggled not to get decimated by the many predatory hyenas and leopards in our precarious corner of Africa. Then, some 60,000 years ago, in what has been termed the great leap forward, we underwent an extraordinary – albeit outwardly invisible – mutation in our minds (what scientists think of as an increase in the number of connections between brain cells) that made us, within a few short generations, the most powerful creature the planet had yet seen.

What fundamentally changed is that we learnt how to learn. Developments in our cerebral cortex meant that we could transmit lessons across generations. A whole tribe became able to benefit from the pioneering developments of its brightest members. Good ideas – about hunting, building, tool-making – did not have to perish along with each one of their individual innovators at every generational juncture.

However bright they might be, all other animals have been denied this luxury. Progressive improvement is not an option for them. They cannot benefit from each other's talents. The vast majority have to survive solely on the instincts hardwired into them. The few that do teach each other things (whales, polar bears) do so only within small family groups; the lessons never go further than from mum to pup. And while they may have a version of language, this is closer to what we would call mime than the fluid, symbolically rich tool we command. It may be possible to communicate to somone via simple signals that there is a predator to their left; but that won't be any use when it's a question of trying to tell them how to assemble a trap, wire a computer or organise an air traffic control system.

It turns out that education lies at the heart of the human advantage. It's why we're not in the zoo. But our very success only begs questions. If we have been so good at teaching one another things in certain areas, why do we remain so profoundly bone-headed in others? Why have we not become one jot either kinder or wiser since the ancient Sumerians? Why, despite all the divorces and bitterness, are we still so bad at relationships – on which 80 percent of a person's lifetime chances of satisfaction depend? Why are we still so filled with anxiety and despair?

We have been astonishingly effective teachers of lessons in how to survive and kill. Real progress will mean finally one day learning how to teach one another how to thrive and love. That will be the true great leap forward.

Christopher Columbus arrives in
America. Engraving by Theodor de Bry
from *Collected travels in the east
Indies and west Indies*, 1594

8.

Few things show up how poor we have collectively been as historians than what happened when Christopher Columbus made landfall on the island of San Salvador (known to the Indigenous inhabitants as Guanahani) on 12 October 1492. The question on everyone's mind – and on both sides – was: who on Earth are these monsters? The local Tainos imagined that the peculiar creatures wearing odd breeches and barbaric feathered hats might be (variously) deities, devils or some kind of hitherto unknown speaking animal. The Europeans imagined that the largely naked locals might be (variously) descendants of Adam and Eve, angels, ogres – or some kind of hitherto unknown speaking animal. What both sides forgot is that they were – of course – very close family.

Every human alive today can be genetically traced back to the same small tribe of *Homo sapiens* that once dwelt in Africa – and from which we are separated by a mere 2,000 generations. Columbus and the Tainos were – in effect – meeting near relatives. Our difficulty is that we forgot who was in the family. Some 125,000 years ago, a group of us got restless and started moving out of our original African habitats. We reached the Middle East 100,000 years ago. Some of us made it to Europe 45,000 years ago, Australia 50,000 years ago, and the Americas 15,000 years ago. We crossed oceans on canoes, walked over the marshy Bering Straits and trekked laboriously across vast ice sheets. For a while, we kept each other in mind. There would have been a family living in another valley who had announced plans to head north; another would have mentioned an idea of trying their luck on the sea. We'd have wondered whatever came of them and perhaps the occasional bit of news would have filtered back. Gradually, we lost touch completely. We forgot the lot that went off to Europe or that were last seen tackling the Arabian desert. The last person who still remembered the old neighbours died and their great-great-grandchildren omitted to mention them to their children. And so, in time, because no one was as yet writing anything down, we had no more memories of our family in the four corners of the Earth. Not only that, but when some of us eventually built big ships and rediscovered them, we had the bad manners to take them for beasts and to try to kill them off with boundless ferocity.

All those fateful meetings with so-called monsters – Hernán Cortés with the Aztecs in 1519, Francisco Pizarro with the Incas in 1531, Jacques Cartier with the Mi'kmaq people in the Gulf of St Lawrence in 1534, Captain Samuel Wallis with the Tahitians in 1767, James Cook with the Aborigines at Kurnell in 1770 – were only re-meetings between peoples too forgetful to remember that their forebears had all known each other in Africa only a little (in the context of geological time) while back.

Talk of the family of humanity may sound like sentimental nonsense poured over a more primal wound of enmity and prejudice. It turns out to be the most hard-headed of all scientific concepts. We really are all brothers and sisters. Tribalism isn't only bad manners; it's extremely poor history.

III.

The Ancients

Marcel-Noël Lambert, *Acropole
d'Athènes*, 1877

1.

No doubt, not every day would have been perfect in Athens during her so-called golden age (c. 500–300 BCE). There would have been moments of squabbling, prejudice and ugliness, and sometimes a sense that things might have been better long ago – or perhaps somewhere else. The sun would not always have shone bright and high in the clear blue Attic skies.

Nevertheless, in so far as humans ever manage to harness their strengths and bring their maddeningly vast (though normally latent) potential to fruition, then it was in the tiny city-state of Athens, during a rare 200-year span that has obsessed and haunted the world's imagination ever since. Whether in 18th-century France or 19th-century Germany, in the minds of artists, philosophers or millions of ordinary travellers, the dream of Athens has generated sighs and longings as few other eras and places ever have.

What has 'the idea of Greece' (as it became known during the Enlightenment) been about? Partly, and not as stupidly as this might initially sound, the weather. This has been a dream fed in part by sunshine. Much of the history of Western civilisation has unfolded in extremely inhospitable and dispiriting climates: that of Berlin and London, Edinburgh and Boston – places where one is guaranteed greyness and rain three-quarters of the year. Athenian civilisation flowered, by contrast, in a climate that bolsters our best sides: an ideal weather for thinking, for looking at things clearly, for taking pride in appearances and recovering hope.

Athens' claims to greatness rest on its superlative devotion to two ideas in particular: beauty, what the Greeks called κάλλο (*kallos*); and wisdom, σοφία (*sophía*). When it came to the first, the Greeks focused on the beauty of nature (the cypress trees, the sea, the olive groves), the beauty of their temples and theatres – and the beauty of the many athletes and gods whose physiques their sculptors never stopped highlighting. And then came wisdom: the brave, undaunted intellectual explorations of their early scientists, the practical, jargon-free, wholly relevant advice of their philosophers and the humane teachings of Homer and the great tragedians, which provided us with an eternally valid map of certain hard-to-reach parts of our psyches.

Most of those who have fallen in love with ancient Athens have not been very good historians. They have – more than anything else – fallen for an *idea* of the place that has emphasised certain aspects and downplayed others. It sounds problematic, but being highly selective about what parts of a civilisation one is interested in may be no error or crime if, in doing so, we are developing our thoughts about ourselves and our needs. We don't have to care about every nuance of Greek history to be hugely enriched by our explorations of it. We can, as people have been doing for hundreds of years, use Athens as a tool for igniting and developing the most important question of all: with the example of the brief history of this small city-state in mind, how might we ideally want to live?

Aphrodite of Cnidus. Marble, 1st–2nd
century CE. Roman copy of a Greek
original by Praxiteles, 4th century BCE

2

We may have seen her so many times before – almost without meaning to – in magazine adverts, on the sides of buses and on postcards, that it can take an effort (as with the *Mona Lisa* or Botticelli's *Venus*) to recover an idea of the originality and freedom-of-mind she represents. To make a vast generalisation: human beings have not – on the whole – been very good observers or appreciators of their own bodies, to go by the evidence bequeathed to us by art. Most of the depictions we have of ourselves show us gaunt, thin, stooped or swaddled coyly in high-necked outfits. The Greeks – unusually and triumphantly – took all their clothes off and showed us what we look like in the full glare of an unembarrassed sun.

Though she is made of stone and the original model died centuries ago, we can at once recognise the Aphrodite of Knidos (or Cnidus) as someone we know. The weight on her ankles, the musculature of her stomach, the slope of her shoulders, these are all entirely and almost eerily familiar to us; we can believe in her reality in a way we seldom can in any artistic figure before the invention of photography. She is so convincing that seeing her can make us oddly melancholy at the thought that someone so alive should, after all, in fact, be long dead.

Very strangely, she is also a goddess. Unlike all those other phantasmagorical figures from other cultures (gods with many arms or the heads of bulls or cats), the Greeks thought it was eminently good enough for their gods to look like all of us. One might be the god of fire or of reason, of wine or (as in this case) of love, one might command the heavens or have power over the seas, and still for all that look identical to someone we might see putting out loungers at the beach or stacking shelves in a bookshop. There is an important message here about self-acceptance: without arrogance, the Greeks believed that being human was far and away a god-like enough achievement. While honouring their deities, they were simultaneously sending a very flattering message to their believers.

We have not, individually and societally, been very good at looking at ourselves with pride. It can, especially after a certain age, be hard to contemplate our reflections without disgust. We can't blame it all on Christianity. Even if there had never been such a religion, there is a deep temptation in the human mind to turn against the flesh and deem it sinful and shameful – and believe that its habits and desires may be inherently corrupt. It takes intellectual effort, and the right sort of coaxing, to imagine that we could take pleasure in the curve of our bottom or to note the impressive articulacy of our wrist. This is most likely to happen in the early days of love; a partner's kind and enthusiastic gaze can persuade us that we do not – after all – always have to be contemptuous of and sickened by our appearance.

The ancient Greeks have – in this respect – acted like lovers to the whole of humanity. Repeatedly they have told us that there is nothing loathsome or shameful about our form. They have opened our eyes to the beauty of thighs, ankles, elbows and shoulder blades. They have urged us to look at ourselves squarely under the brightest daylight – and enjoy who we are.

The Lancellotti Discobolus. Marble, 2nd
century CE. Roman copy of a Greek bronze
original by Myron, 5th century BCE

3

What is distinctive about the ancient Greeks is not so much that they did sport with immense and influential enthusiasm; it's what they imagined that sport could be combined with.

Our own era also takes sport very seriously: athletes command vast sums, sporting fixtures are staples of broadcasting, equipment manufacturers vaunt the benefits of active lifestyles. Yet we show our lack of imagination and generosity in the sort of mental or psychological life that we imply that an athlete might plausibly have. We place our athletes firmly in one corner and our intellectuals, poets and artists in another. We would be extremely surprised if one of our top discus throwers turned out to be, simultaneously, a professor of philosophy, and we would surely start to think less of a historian or astronomer who – it emerged – spent a good part of every day at the gym.

The Greeks held no such prejudices. For them, a devotion to perfecting the body went hand in hand with an interest in developing the mind. Apollo, the god of Reason, was not coincidentally always depicted as extremely athletic, with a well-developed torso and calves of the sort of firmness that require hours of training. The greatest wrestler of antiquity, Milo of Croton (six times winner of the famous Pythian Games at Delphi), had a second career as a celebrated Pythagorean philosopher. Many of Plato's dialogues are set in the gym, where Socrates and his companions discuss the greatest questions of the intellect while working on their chests and legs. A 'gymnasium' was not, as it is for us, a place filled with weights and bench presses; it was a centre of discussion and learning that happened also to have some sporting facilities attached to it.

The Greeks venerated exercise because of their respect for the sort of thinking one can be capable of after vigorous training: nimble, unpretentious, sprightly and filled with daring. They would have worried not so much about the health as about the mental vigour of intellectuals who felt tired after a walk around the block or never dared to enter a competitive race. They refused to countenance a division between mind and body: they didn't want exercise to be stupid, but they also didn't want thinking to be out of shape and weak-spirited. It was their distinctive genius to perceive a mutual dependence between athletics and philosophy.

The Greeks continue to offer us a challenge: it isn't enough just to be clever, nor is it right to be merely brawny. They refused our later disastrous dichotomies. They wanted beauty to help wisdom, and strength to assist intelligence. They wanted clever people to think about how they were breathing and running; and beautiful people to worry about what they were reading. There can be few of us who won't feel that we have some adjustment to make in the light of their rich example.

The Antimenes Painter, black-figure
amphora featuring a painting of olive-
gathering, Attica, Greece, 520 BCE

4

The ancient Greeks distinguished themselves by their manner of *thinking*. They managed to be at once very highbrow and extremely practical. They are exemplars of what a society of farmers and fishermen can produce when, after a few generations, some of them leave their groves and nets behind and turn their minds to figuring out what love or justice are, or what might make existence meaningful.

They had the advantage of being early to the game. Few people had been on the territory before and so they could carve their original paths across virgin snow. They were not hampered – as we so often are – by an intimidating worry as to 'what others might previously have thought'. There had been no others, or no one that they knew about. So they could have a first shot at raising the truly enormous questions that most of us shy away from out of a belief that someone, somewhere has surely done better than we ever could with them: what is education for? Why do we fall in love with certain people but not others? How should governments be arranged so as to limit people's irrational sides? The Greek thinkers were as fresh and undaunted as children – with the tough, careful minds of adults.

We often excuse the paucity of our own thinking by claiming that we have not yet 'read enough'. The Greeks would laugh at our self-pity from across the generations: we have all already read a great deal more than Plato or Aristotle. We know so much more than Homer or Euripides. The predominant share of intelligence has nothing to do with how much one has read and everything to do with how deeply one is able to think an issue through cleanly in one's own mind.

The Greeks were marked by a desire to link intellectual exploration to practical outcomes. They didn't want to be 'clever' so much as wise. They wanted to put their ideas to work in the course of everyday life. This was – after all – the society that kept telling itself the story of the distinguished astrologer Thales from Miletus, who was so busy looking at the stars that he tripped and fell into a ditch. Or a society whose leading philosopher, Epicurus, could declare:

Vain is the word of a philosopher, which does not heal any suffering of man. For just as there is no profit in medicine if it does not expel the diseases of the body, so there is no profit in philosophy if it does not expel the suffering of the mind.

Greek thinkers learnt to make their writings brief, clear and charming to ordinary busy audiences. They got to the point very fast – and with a concern for entertainment. They tried to sound interesting rather than merely clever. The originality of the dramatic form in which Plato wrote his dialogues, mixing banter and jokes with metaphysical reflection, hasn't been surpassed to this day: it was as if Heidegger or Kant had teamed up with the creators of a soap opera to deliver disquisitions on existential questions in a tavern.

And lastly, the Greek thinkers saw no opposition between being intelligent and being commercial. Plato and Aristotle were canny businessmen, setting up lucrative schools of life, the Academy and the Lyceum respectively, to spread their teachings and earn them money. They understood that the ultimate proof of whether your thinking has reached its mark and made a difference is when ordinary people want to pay for it – just as, at the market, they might purchase a swordfish or a jar of olives. It's easy enough to dazzle people with ideas; it's a greater challenge still to prompt them to want to pay real money for them.

Odysseus (tied to the mast of
his ship) and the Sirens, detail
from a mosaic depicting scenes from
Homer's *Odyssey*, 'House of Ulysses',
Dougga, Tunisia, 3rd century CE

5.

It can be tempting to glaze over at the mention of 'Greek myths'. Too many of us have been scarred by early encounters with them in the classroom. Our minds are often (helpfully) focused on what we need to survive – and our boredom with Greek mythology is telling us with some vehemence that there doesn't appear to be anything here we could possibly use for ourselves.

Stories 'work' (that is, interest and do something for us) when – even though they may be describing specific people in particular settings – they manage to illuminate, consciously or less so, aspects of our own dilemmas and desires. And that is ultimately how the best Greek stories have worked. Beneath a layer of local colour, they teach us about ourselves. Aesop's fables aren't – for example – narrowly about a tortoise and a hare or an ant and a grasshopper. Nor is the narrative of Daedalus and Icarus about a peculiar ancient aeronautical misadventure, nor is the tale of Tantalus – caught between tempting grapes and nourishing waters forever out of reach – about some unpleasant politics among the gods. These are stories that concern us and people we know.

The situation is no different with that often off-puttingly grand-seeming masterpiece of Greek literature, Homer's *Odyssey*. Beneath the intimidating exterior, one of its greatest themes is something we all know about: temptation. The Greeks were obsessed with how easy it is to be led astray from one's commitments; they called the problem *akrasia*, or weakness of will, and observed how Odysseus constantly knows what he should do while being visited by contrary temptations and appetites, mostly related to sex, pride and vanity. He is, despite his armour and unusual name and knowledge of seafaring, a version of each of us, committed at heart to making it back to Penelope and Ithaca, but prone to being trapped by monsters, seduced by gods, provoked by serpents and caught up in whirlpools.

When Odysseus finally decides that enough is enough and that he must sail home past an isle filled with the haunting presence of beautiful sirens, he does so while tied to the mast of his ship and with his ears blocked with wax. It's a lesson in how we, too, might cope with rabid temptations.

Fine arguments may ultimately get us nowhere. We may need to take simple blunt precautions: lock the cupboard, throw away the phone and refuse to see a particular friend ever again.

Each of us will have slightly different sirens and slightly different Ithacas: those universal concepts generously birthed from the imaginations of the Greeks will fly under local banners and colours. They might be called Michelle and computing or Trevor and business school, but we can be sure that we will have them and that we will see more clearly into them while following in the turbulent wake of Odysseus' ship.

Jan Brueghel the Elder, *A Fantastic
Cave with Odysseus and Calypso*, 1616

6

It can be easy to form an impression that Greek women occupied an exceptionally subservient position in their society. They couldn't vote, nor inherit property; they were barred from public office and denied a proper education. These were genuine ills, but few men at an individual or collective level have ever tried to veil or repress women without having experience, or a great and underlying terror, of their strength.

The Greeks, for all the evident gender inequality of their societies, despite a host of legal and financial strictures, were unusual in the intensity with which they recognised and honoured the power that women can exercise over men, for good and ill. Greek art and myths are filled with women who defy the structures built by men to try to contain them: Artemis, Athena, Hestia, Medea, Phaedra ...

Female power is never more evident than in the central story of Greek civilisation. In Homer's *Odyssey*, one of the strongest, bravest warriors of all time has his life upturned by a succession of women. On his way back to his home and wife, Odysseus makes landfall on the shores of the island of Aeaea, owned by the goddess Circe, who can turn the very strongest and noblest of men into pigs; there could be few more psychologically telling transformations, given that around women, this is often precisely what some of us are or, perhaps, fear to become. Odysseus narrowly escapes such a fate, but Circe is lonely and forces him to stay for a couple of years and have two children with her.

When he eventually makes his escape, it's only to wind up – a short time later – on the island of Ogygia, owned by the no less powerful nymph Calypso. She, too, wants Odysseus to stay and does her best to persuade him, by offering him a flower-filled bower, food and beautiful music. The relationship lasts seven years. It takes all of Odysseus' fragile will to dare eventually to explain to Calypso that he truly needs to head on, that he must get back to Ithaca, that he has a son to see and a wife he still loves and lands to look after. Calypso's ensuing fury is every bit as terrifying as the fighter had feared. He is lucky to get away alive.

No man, however outwardly strong he might appear, can get through his life without having to negotiate from a position of subservience with a dominant woman. As men unconsciously know, we were all one day helpless infants at the mercy of a mother. The Greeks understood and respected the ensuing power dynamics. They looked with pity and at times gentle mockery at men – and variously with awe and apprehension at women. Few of us are going to need to get back home after fighting a foreign army in a distant city; all of us have lessons we can absorb from the tormented couplings and moral struggles of Odysseus.

Left: The Apollo of the Belvedere,
c. 120-140 CE. Roman copy of a lost
bronze original by Leochares,
4th century BCE
Right: The young Bacchus with
a personification of the vine
(Ampelus), c. 150-200 BCE

7

Few things better demonstrate the ancient Greeks' commitment to balance and emotional integration than their simultaneous worship of two very different gods.

The first was Apollo, the son of Zeus and his mistress Leto, god of reason, calm, foresight, education and the golden mean. Born on the island of Delos, Apollo was said to have been fed as a child with nectar from Themis, goddess of divine law, and this is what gave him his taste for rationality, logic and legal precision. Apollo was the god to whom humans might have turned when they were setting up a new city and wanted to ensure that laws were just and logical. Apollo watched over education. He liked architecture. He was interested in symmetry and balance, peace and moderation. Inscribed on the portico of his Doric temple at Delphi were two characteristically Apollonian commands: 'Nothing in excess' (Μηδὲν ἄγαν) and 'Know thyself' (γνωθι σεαυτόν). This was the god who might preside over clear-minded, purposeful mornings when we are at last able to make progress on important projects that have been delayed for too long.

But there was another god to whom the Greeks were devoted. Dionysus, son of Zeus and Persephone, was the god of wine, dancing, theatre, religious ecstasy, festivity and madness. He was celebrated annually at the Festival of Dionysus, in late March or April. For a few days, Athenians would watch plays at the foot of the Acropolis and, most importantly, get extremely drunk and dance through the night in public, usually in the fields and woods outside of the city gates. Dionysus was the god for evenings when the boredom, restraint and self-sacrifice of our routines have grown intolerable.

The Greeks were wise enough to know that a good life cannot be merely reasonable. If we are to remain sane, we have to let madness regularly have its due. We need a chance to release ourselves from the strictures of society, to flail our limbs wildly to the sound of a lyre and beat of a tympanon (a kind of tambourine) and to let copious cups of wine dissolve our inhibitions. For a time, we must be able to say the unsayable; under the stars, we should be as peculiar as we need to be, lost in what the Greeks called ecstasy (from *ekstasis*, ἔκστασις, meaning 'to stand outside of oneself').

With their characteristic prescience, the Greeks put a finger on – and poetically named – two necessary aspects of a good life. We will never achieve anything worthwhile without the blessing of Apollo; we will eventually break down and go mad without regular moments of submission to the frenzied rule of Dionysus.

Pericles's Funeral Oration. Print,
after the painting by Philipp von
Foltz, 1853

8

If there is one thing most modern politicians can agree on, it's that ancient Athens' greatest gift to the world was the concept of democracy. The term derives from the ancient Greek words *dêmos* or δῆμος, meaning 'people', and *krátos* or κράτος, meaning 'power'. With a few interruptions, from roughly 508 to 322 BCE, the city of Athens was governed by the will of its (exclusively male, adult and non-slave) citizenry. Over ten fixed meetings a year, the Assembly (*ekklesía*) would gather and, by a direct show of hands, decide on the central matters of the state. Modern societies have, since their beginnings, been awed by this bold anticipation of their own chosen methods of rule.

In reality, the ancient Greeks did something far more interesting than invent democracy. They arrived at some extremely prescient thoughts on why democracy doesn't quite work – or can at least be extremely problematic. In his *Republic*, Plato describes Socrates falling into conversation with a character called Adeimantus and trying to puncture holes in the basis of democracy by comparing a society to a ship. If you were heading out on a journey by sea, asks Socrates, who would you ideally want to decide who was in charge of the vessel? Just anyone, or people educated in the rules and demands of seafaring? The latter, of course, says Adeimantus. So why then, responds Socrates, do we keep thinking that any old person should be fit to judge who should be a ruler of a country?

Socrates' point is that voting in an election is a skill, not a random intuition. And like any skill, it needs to be taught systematically to people. Letting the citizenry vote without an education is as irresponsible as putting them in charge of a trireme sailing to Samos in a storm.

Democracy is a beautiful idea, but its decisions are often extremely unreasonable – and the Greek philosophers knew it. We will continue to have great difficulties (demagogues, witch hunts, etc.) if we allow everyone to vote before everyone has learnt to think. The Greek anti-democrats didn't believe in withholding the vote from people indefinitely; only until they had been properly schooled. A democratic state can only be as good as its education system – in other words, until now, in most parts of the world, not very good at all.

The best of the Greeks knew the answer we still grapple with: that there should be no representation without a superlative education.

The Ancient Theatre of Epidaurus,
Peloponnese, Greece, 4th century BCE

9

Every society tries to explain for itself the question of why people fail: the Greeks were distinctive in inventing a whole new art form to do so.

Tragic art began in the theatres of ancient Greece in the 6th century BCE and followed a hero, usually a high-born one, a king or a famous warrior, from prosperity and acclaim to ruin and shame – through some error or oversight of his own. (Translated into our own age, this would have been like an art form that exclusively told stories about the slips and falls of CEOs, head teachers, military generals, celebrities or top politicians.) Aristotle, the great analyst of tragedy, made a key observation: in a good tragedy, the error or oversight should be easy for the audience to relate to. Characters shouldn't do something obviously ghastly or violent, just the sort of thing we might be guilty of every day, but normally get away with, thanks to the grace of the gods: a sudden loss of temper, a sexual impulse, a bit of greed or dishonesty, a burst of vanity.

Because of the highly relatable nature of the error, we would be unlikely to respond to a tragic character with moralism or condemna-tion. We wouldn't walk out of a tragedy calling the hero or heroine a 'loser'. Rather, we would be inclined to feel devastation and pity for the unfortunate person whom we had seen ruin-ing their life in a few easy steps – and at the same time a terror for ourselves because of how easily (as we could now see) a basically good person might unleash a nightmare in a few sim-ple moves.

The point of tragedy for the Greeks was to reduce our tendencies to judge harshly and to insist that we would never be capable of this or that piece of bad behaviour; it was to try to render us kinder. By taking us slowly through a story of ruin, the playwrights opened our eyes to how near we are to a precipice at all times.

Nowadays, most of our tragic stories are told to us by newspapers. These are the organs we entrust with the details of domestic murders, corporate downfalls and moments of madness, and they invariably seek to sell us a very un-Greek moral: that the people who fail are bad, evil, sinful and deserve what's happened to them. They are 'perverts', 'weirdoes' and 'sickoes'. The ancient Greeks were a great deal more advanced. They could not forget, and sought always to remind us, of a daunting, beautiful and almost unbearable truth: *that wrong doesn't exclusively occur to the bad; that good people fail.*

Caspar de Crayer, *Alexander and Diogenes*, c. 1625–1630

10

The ancients were fond – for reasons that tell us much about their nature – of a story about one of the most powerful men in the world and a penniless philosopher. According to legend, Alexander the Great, King of Macedon, founder of the greatest empire yet known (it stretched from Greece to north-western India), happened to be visiting the city of Corinth, where there lived a philosopher called Diogenes of Sinope. Diogenes belonged to the Cynic school of philosophy, which questioned prevailing social norms and refused to bow to authority. The philosopher had for a number of years been living in a large ceramic jar (a *pithos*) in the marketplace to show how little he cared for material goods. He had a habit of provoking his fellow citizens with a range of stunts: he had a lamp he liked to carry in broad daylight, and when asked why, would reply that he was looking for an honest man.

The philosopher Plutarch recounts what happened when Alexander met Diogenes:

Thereupon many statesmen and philosophers came to Alexander with their congratulations, and he expected that Diogenes of Sinope also, who was tarrying in Corinth, would do likewise. But since that philosopher took not the slightest notice of Alexander, and continued to enjoy his leisure in the suburb of Craneion, Alexander went in person to see him, and he found him lying in the sun. Diogenes raised himself up a little when he saw so many people coming towards him, and fixed his eyes upon Alexander. And when that monarch addressed him with greetings, and asked if he wanted anything, 'Yes,' said Diogenes, 'stand a little out of my sun.' It is said that Alexander was so struck by this, and admired so much the haughtiness and grandeur of the man who had nothing but scorn for him, that he said to his followers, who were laughing and jesting about the philosopher as they went away,

'But truly, if I were not Alexander, I wish I were Diogenes.'

Alexander in this story stands for everything our society tells us we are supposed to want to be: a tech billionaire, a famous film star, a famed environmentalist. And Diogenes is the exemplar of independence and self-determination. Few of us aspire to live in storage jars; Diogenes is pointing us to the virtues of paying more attention to our intimate needs and less to fashion and popular opinion. A modern Diogenes might conclude that they hated the friends they'd grown up with, that they wanted to give up their job in order to teach Medieval music to children, were going to throw away their phones and loathed the prevailing social orthodoxies.

Most of our time is spent bowing to power and aligning ourselves with the majority. The Greeks understood – via Diogenes – that our ultimate loyalty should be to our own hearts, in all their striking strangeness and awkwardness.

The ruins of the 4th-century BCE
theatre at Megalopoli, Central
Peloponnese, Greece; in the
background, a coal-burning power
station

11

One of the most dispiriting experiences for lovers of ancient Greece who visit the modern country is to note how little of the greatness they perceived has survived in pristine or impressive form into the present day. The old ruins lie scattered among motorways and power stations. 4th-century BCE theatres look out onto supermarkets and water parks. Few people remember the old philosophers or playwrights; the airwaves are dominated by mass media that trivialise and demean topics; all the errors of democracy are on display. Nothing much has been learnt.

If we feel drawn to ancient Greek culture, we're typically advised to fly to Athens, acquire a decent guidebook, visit the Acropolis and its associated museum, travel to some of the key temples at Delphi or at Delos – and then go home *and sigh*. Sigh at the contrast between a golden age that is lost and our own squalid times; sigh because Athens can never be rebuilt.

It sounds sensible, but this is a counsel of despair. We should travel to Greece not passively to admire, as tourists do, but to steal as political reformers can. We should use Greece as a practical template for how to build a better world for ourselves right now. Four big suggestions come to the fore:

1. Architecture
Inspired by the Greeks, we should build cities that are not only efficient and prosperous but, more than anything, beautiful. It isn't about creating pastiche Classical buildings, but about emulating the dignity and harmony of Greek architecture (even in modern forms and materials). We will have reached a stage of true civilisation when politicians emerge who declare that they want to build not only a fairer or more environmentally sensitive world, but first and foremost, an architecturally more beautiful one.

2. Democracy
We should buttress a democratic voting system with exceptional investment in education. The Greeks were pre-eminent educators, but they made only the first moves. Encouraged by Plato's Academy and Aristotle's Lyceum, we should exploit all media to promulgate teachings related to the pursuit of what the Greeks called *eudaimonia* or 'flourishing' We should teach in schools but – far more importantly – also in gyms and around athletics tracks.

3. Tragedy
We should – through the skilful use of mass media – generate an atmosphere of sophisticated tolerance towards all those who unwittingly make errors and fail. We should use art to teach kindness.

4. Philosophy
We should ensure that philosophers are not merely holed up in obscure academies teaching things that no one has any investment in, but rather out in public squares challenging public opinion, refining ideas and helping us to find harmony and consolation.

We pay ancient Greece the ultimate homage when we cease looking at it as a touristic artefact and view it instead as providing part of the template to a world we need to build today.

Remains of the aqueducts Aqua
Claudia and Anio Novus (both 52 CE)
integrated into the Aurelian Wall
(271 CE), Rome, Italy

12

Few things feel as relevant, touching and relatable about the Romans as their profound interest in bathing and pooing. There may be other highpoints of Roman civilisation (the arches and temples, the literature, the military conquests, the legal system), but none feel as visceral as these.

Rome's first aqueduct, the Aqua Appia, was built in 312 BCE; by the 3rd century CE, Rome had eleven aqueducts bringing 900,000 cubic metres of fresh water a day into a city of a million people. The head of the water supply, known as the Curator Acquarum, held one of the most prestigious and well-rewarded positions in Rome, and was a direct appointee of the emperor. There were close to a thousand baths throughout the capital. Some were in private hands, and others – like the vast public baths of Diocletian – could hold 3,000 people and were centres of immense civic pride (as well as of learning, recreation, exercise and networking).

Pooing was taken as seriously: Rome's main sewage pipe, the Cloaca Maxima, was built as early as the 4th century BCE and was upgraded and expanded throughout the Roman era. Above ground, luxurious public rooms, decorated with elaborate frescoes, typically of gardens and birds, allowed one plentiful time to sit on marble latrines, perhaps with a book rented from a nearby library. In his *Natural History*, the Roman historian Pliny the Elder remarked that of all the things Romans had ever accomplished (and he knew most of the list), the sewers were 'the most noteworthy things of all'. Modern historians tend to date the conclusive end of Roman civilisation to 537 CE, when the Ostrogoth king Vitiges finally disconnected and destroyed Rome's aqueduct system.

Logically underpinning these masterpieces of engineering was a particular receptivity to the body and its pleasures and pains: the Romans were unusually sensorily alive, and that's why they became hydrological engineers of genius. A predominantly religious civilisation might devote the greatest share of its intelligence and resources to celebrating a feeling of awe in the presence of the divine, and mark its time on Earth with the construction of a Chartres Cathedral or a Dome of the Rock. The Romans, by contrast, channelled an uncommon degree of their wealth and ingenuity into the distinctive pleasures of lolling at length in a pool of piping hot water – and so made their bid for immortality by putting up the Antonine Baths at Carthage and the Baths of Trajan in Rome. In honour of nothing more nor less than the feeling afforded by fresh linen on clean skin and of a comfortable bowel movement, they spent 30 million sesterces on the immense Nîmes Aqueduct, 50 kilometres long and, at the famous Pont du Gard bridge, 48 metres high. In calling the Romans 'pagans', what we ultimately mean is that they valued a powerful body scrub far above any transport of the soul. It would be about fourteen centuries after the demise of their civilisation before one could have a decent bath anywhere in the West again.

It takes a special kind of intelligence to hold on to what actually makes us content – even when this might be easy to mock or trivialise. The Romans never forgot the claims of their bodies. We should be moved by – and feel a sense of intimate kinship with – all those who worry at length about finding a pleasant toilet and locate their chief source of consolation in a long, hot bath.

Roman road, Blackstone Edge,
Rishworth Moor, near Manchester,
England, c. 120 CE

13

The Romans were manically and beautifully predictable. They always put up the same sort of temples to Jupiter and Minerva; they always laid down mosaics showing the head of Medusa or a lion chasing a bull; they always built the same sort of amphitheatres from Dyrrhachium in Albania to Aventicum in Switzerland; they always relied on either Doric, Ionic or Corinthian columns in their civic buildings; and their roads always had similar kinds of flagstones and drainage ditches, whether these were running across a moor in 1st-century Britannia or an olive grove in 2nd-century Cappadocia. Across 5 million square kilometres of empire, the Romans kept doing more or less the same thing for close to 500 years.

As a result, whether one visits Trier in southwestern Germany or Kotayk province in central Armenia, Meknes in Morocco or Aswan in Egypt, Tyne and Wear in northern England or Segovia in Spain, one can count on coming across near-identical bits of Roman civilisation: a denarius with the head of Marcus Aurelius or an aureus with the bust of Plotina; a villa with colonnades and an *impluvium* (rainwater pool); some *tabernae* and *thermopolia* (shops and take-aways); the remains of a theatre and a chunk of an aqueduct.

We're used to thinking ill of globalisation. What is universal is – almost invariably – the worst of our mindsets: the demeaning television programmes, the ugly international hotels, the soulless corporations, the tacky chain stores, the sickening fast foods.

The Romans, too, were internationalists – but they present us with a different vision of what the term might mean. They wished to banish homesickness by bringing the very finest and most elevating elements of home with them wherever they travelled. It might be 10° below zero on the border with Caledonia and, across the defensive lines, barbarians might be sleeping in the skins of wolves and eating black barley porridge laced with offal, but the Romans knew they were never far from a pistachio and fava bean salad, a soundly heated room and a volume of Cicero's essays.

In reaction to our degenerate vision of internationalism, it has been tempting to insist on localism. We celebrate everything folkloric and provincial. We insist on our buildings being different on every street corner, on our currencies altering every time we cross a border and on our laws failing to harmonise across landmasses. We would be insulted to travel across the world and eat the same food and sleep in an identical bed.

The Romans provide us with inspiration to escape this dichotomy. With their examples in mind, we might stop our architects from going back to the drawing board every time they received a commission – and simply give them eight or so outstanding models to work from, whatever the occasion or locale. Theatres might look nearly identical from Sydney to Calgary. We should insist on one sort of road design and one kind of currency, one way of laying out a house and one approach to entertainment. So long as what is international is outstanding, we will be enhanced rather than reduced by global similarity. Chain hotels or stores do not have to define what we understand by an international spirit.

The Romans remind us that it is never globalisation that we mind, only the degenerate form of it that our architects, lawyers, chefs, road designers, educators and plumbers have to date managed to concoct. Looking 'the same as everywhere else' should, in a better future world, come to sound like the very highest form of praise.

Flora, goddess of flowers and spring,
in a wall painting from the Villa
di Arianna in Stabiae near Pompeii,
Italy, 1st century CE

14

Given how diverse the world is and how many forces act upon it, it seems rather peculiar that humans should ever have arrived at the idea of *one* god: an extremely busy character who must be responsible for everything from the colour of hummingbirds to the ebb and flow of tides to the nature of our exam results and the health of our brother-in-law. We might be hard pressed to guess that it was monotheism that historically won out over, and is commonly viewed as a more mature successor to, polytheism. To pay homage to a number of gods seems a great deal more charming, useful and in its own way logical than insisting – with stubborn vehemence – on the need to obey one fellow alone.

More sophisticated than us in so many ways, the Romans came to favour a broad pantheon. They were in the habit of absorbing pretty much any god from any territory they conquered and so ended up – at the peak of their empire – with an assortment of over 200 gods (Jesus was, in the early days, simply – and sensibly – just another one to add to the list). Their gods included – to give one a sense of the range – Sterquilinus, god of manure, Mellona, god of honey, Fontus, god of springs and wells, Ops, goddess of fertility, Fides, goddess of trust and good faith, Flora, goddess of flowers and spring, Vejovis, god of healing, Cardea, goddess of door hinges, Fabulinus, god of children's reading ability, Fessona, goddess of siestas and Terminus, god of borders and boundary markers.

In pretty much any situation, whenever there was something beautiful to celebrate or worrying to fend off, Romans had a very specific god to turn to. Couples who were squabbling could pray to Manturna, goddess of marital reconciliation; a farmer worried about his apple harvest could implore Vertumnus, god of fruit trees; someone who was finding sex tricky could say a word to Volupia, goddess of orgasms – and a labourer dreading toil in the fields could beg for mercy from Spiniensis, god of thorns and thistles.

The presence of so many gods respects the multifaceted nature of life. We tend to require targeted assistance, and a broad range of gods gives us a specific figure to petition: a god for flat tyres, a god for maddening teenagers, a god for delayed planes … Knowing that a god is in total charge of a restricted province allows prayers to be focused and hopes accurately targeted. It also means that, rather than hosting a muddle of the randomly desperate, Roman temples were able to sift their audiences: one only for mothers with difficulty breastfeeding, another only for householders with squeaky hinges. There was a chance to share precise sorrows and exchange granular advice.

Religion isn't only about asking for things, of course, it's also about saying thank you. Here, too, polytheism has its advantages. A god uniquely responsible for honey or safe journeys or coughs seems a better divinity to express thanks to than an all-purpose spirit likely to be the recipient of millions of chaotic messages of gratitude. At a shrine to a god of apricots or of comfortable shoes, a believer becomes akin to the audience of a work of art, who is sensitised to the wonders of a small but vital aspect of life by the evocative talents of a painter or photographer.

The Romans did not appear terrified of their gods; there were too many of them, their characters were too varied and their responsibilities too scattered. They were largely benevolent figures, always ready to help out in return for a modest offering and in competition with one another for our attention and care.

Roman polytheism may yet turn out to be an ideal faith for those who don't believe in – and may have little interest in – religion, but who still seek an occasional home for feelings of gratitude, longing and despair.

Façade of the Library of Celsus in
Ephesus, Turkey, 2nd century CE

15.

Like the ancient Greeks, the Romans cleaved to an admirably practical view of learning. A person's reasons for reading books or for becoming a philosopher or a historian were envisaged as pragmatic and goal-oriented; learning was definitely not for learning's sake. People learnt in order to understand suffering, to calm their spirits and to live and die well.

Gaius Julius Aquila was a high-ranking Roman official and consul who around 115 CE bequeathed a very large sum – 25,000 denarii – to build a library in memory of his father, Tiberius Julius Celsus Polemaeanus, in the city of Ephesus in modern Turkey. At the time, Ephesus was second only to Rome in importance and elegance. Aquila had been a man of the world and he intended his library to collect together all knowledge – some 16,000 scrolls – that a person might require to navigate the challenges of existence successfully.

Aquila also knew that unless his vision of knowledge was presented with sufficient architectural skill and artistic conviction, it would get lost amidst the many less elevated distractions of Ephesus. So Aquila had the façade of his Library of Celsus decorated in a grand style. Between four pairs of composite columns, he placed statues of the four virtues held by the Greeks to underpin a well-governed life: Episteme (knowledge), Ennoia (intelligence), Arete (excellence) – and, most importantly, Sophia (wisdom). Inside, at the top of a reading room covered in delicate carved acanthus leaves, to further emphasise the point of the building, visitors looked up to see a statue of Minerva, Roman goddess of wisdom.

It has been rare in history for those who possess worldly power to take much of an interest in wisdom; seldom have statues of Sophia or Minerva been given pride of place in buildings that equal law courts or temples in scale and beauty. Plenty of Romans devoted their excess wealth to luxury and popular entertainment, plenty blew it on wine and gladiator contests, but there were a few like Aquila who concluded that the best possible use for their resources lay in creating temples for the mind. Importantly, Aquila's building was not a research institute or university in the modern sense, but a therapeutic centre of learning open to everyone, where books were arranged to offer counsel and consolation and occasions for reflection and edification.

There are few Aquilas still at large with 10,000 or 20,000 denarii to spare. The Library of Celsus was destroyed in a fire in 262 CE; the world awaits its successors, comparably elegant buildings that could combine great architecture with ideas in a way that could assist us in our efforts to remain sane, calm and good.

Wall painting from the imperial
villa at Boscotrecase, Naples, Italy,
1st century BCE

16

Many past civilisations, when their documents are recovered and their fragments are dug out of the ground and arranged in museums, are capable of generating feelings of awe, wonder and renewed perspective. Yet few of them act upon us as the ruins of ancient Rome are inclined to do. Few create a spontaneous, vivid, direct sense that we would like to go back and live right there with them; that this – despite the centuries and certain gaps in understanding – is where one's true home lies.

Seldom are such nostalgic feelings liable to be more powerful than in relation to the villa at Boscotrecase, at the foot of Mount Vesuvius, buried in the eruption of 79 CE, that once belonged to a Roman aristocrat, Agrippa, friend of the emperor Augustus and husband of his daughter Julia.

The house may have lacked a few of the amenities we would now take for granted, but not very many. Like almost all Roman elite dwellings, it had an atrium at the front where residents met guests and took the air. A shallow basin at the centre (the *impluvium*) caught rainwater in a reflecting pool. Off the atrium were bedrooms, offices, a kitchen and bathrooms – and at the back there was a colonnaded garden with a pond. There was underfloor heating and running water. The walls were done up with exquisitely delicate and light frescoes, on which narrow vertical bands framed scenes from nature and mythology.

The nicest bedroom in the villa – and possibly in the ancient or in fact in any world – was located to the rear of the house. Overlooking the Bay of Naples, it was done up in Mark Rothko's favourite colours: black, deep purple and the occasional band of gold. In the centre of each panel was a tiny landscape, floating like an island in the blackness.

We might explain our attraction to the room purely on the grounds of common aesthetic tastes, but the congruence may be deeper: it is because we long for the same sorts of things in life. Our favoured style of beauty hints at a shared vision of happiness. Like us, the Romans wanted calm, because they had created a world whose clamour they could no longer control. Like us, they craved sensitivity and delicacy, because so much about public life could be bewildering. And like us, they dreamt of nature, because they had left so much of it behind.

They would have understood key bits of us and we of them. After they left the scene, we lose the ability to recognise ourselves so easily in their successors: they could be impressive no doubt, these barbarians – with their heavy castles, jewel-encrusted swords and devotions to a single God – but they seem to want unfamiliar things and their bedrooms hint at contrasting sensibilities. It's a privilege of Rome that, beneath its layers of ash and earth, we discover what feel like unusually close long-lost companions with congruent tastes in interior decoration.

Canaletto, *Ruins of the Forum, Looking
towards the Capitol*, 1742

17

The most haunting fact behind the achievement of ancient Rome was that it didn't – in the end – last. Despite every effort of the Imperial government, in spite of incessant defensive wars, attempts at renewal, exhortations, chastisements and sacrifices, the empire fell – and by the 6th century CE, it was a collapsed and derided hulk trampled upon by its many gleeful conquerors and ignored by its indifferent and weary former populations. Its marble was stripped to decorate churches, its treasure was stolen to fund barbarian wars. The Temple of Jupiter Capitolinus was plundered so that only its podium and base survived; the Temple of Saturn was reduced to eight forlorn, roofless columns. Grazing cattle moved into what had been the Forum. Imperial palaces became latrines. Rubbish piled up on top of the shattered remains of theatres and law courts. Books were burnt or their pages were written over with Christian myths.

The story of the destruction has long provided ammunition for a certain side of all of our natures: the side that is prone to despair, that knows that all effort will come to naught. If this massive collective work of ingenuity and beauty fell apart, then what hope is there for anything that we might seek or do? All our striving can feel doomed as we intimate that animals will one day in turn defecate and mewl in our former offices and homes.

Still, when the pessimism has passed, the overwhelming effect of the ruins has been to spur leading minds on to a desire to recreate the glory that once was. Generations of observers have looked at Rome and been devoured by a wish to rebuild as beautifully, to reorder as soundly, to dream on as big a scale. This is why there have been so many attempts at revival, of which the initiative we know as the Renaissance was only the most historically well known.

Yet despite all our Classical initiatives, we are still not there. We may have relearnt to make concrete and lay down underfloor heating. But we have not – arguably – built a world that the Romans would be able to admire as genuinely superior to their own. The original model therefore continues, as it has done for many centuries, to play a central role in guiding our efforts and focusing our thoughts on an ideal future. We will know that we have at last overcome the loss of Rome when we can feel sure that a magically resurrected Roman, someone born in the age of Augustus or Trajan, could look around at the modern world and conclude that we were truly a more advanced and admirable civilisation than the one they had come from. And because on that question, the jury continues to be out, we must, for a while yet, remain Rome's devoted and humble students.

IV.
Christianity

Jean-Baptiste-Siméon Chardin,
The Scullery Maid, c. 1738

1.

The clearest sign of just how influential Christianity has been is – paradoxically – to be found outside of anything distinctly Christian: outside of churches, priests, altars, Bibles, monasteries or rituals. Almost imperceptibly, the religion has shaped the global mind. Whether or not we believe in it, and especially if we do not, the religion has given certain of our thoughts a distinctive tenor. There are ideas and attitudes in circulation that are thoroughly Christian in spirit without ever identifying themselves as such. Christianity's greatest victory has been to make itself feel like common sense.

Central to Christianity has been an argument about the value of ordinary lives. This was a religion whose pivotal figure was born in a stable, worked as a carpenter, was friends with sex workers and died among criminals; this was a religion that never stopped stressing that God's mercy was offered to all irrespective of social status; this was a religion whose first adherents were slaves – and that lent spiritual prestige to meekness and poverty. In the Christian schema, we can lack an education, live in a hut, work as a labourer – and still have a paramount place in the divine order. Without Christianity, modern democracy could never have achieved its supremacy. Without Christianity, there would have been no welfare state, no universal education and no civil rights movement. Christianity's reach can be felt whenever human beings push back against hierarchy and exclusion and emphasise the dignity and legitimacy of every life.

The French 18th-century painter Jean-Baptiste-Siméon Chardin (1699–1779) never produced any explicitly religious works – and nor, as far as we can tell, did he believe. But his paintings are entirely Christian in spirit. They take us into kitchens and back rooms, parlours and yards, and introduce us to servants, cooks and maids at work preparing meals, darning clothes and caring for children. There is no overt moralising; we aren't told that the poor might be the first to enter the Kingdom of Heaven or that the meek are especially blessed; there is no specific mention of the Sermon on the Mount.

There doesn't need to be. We get the idea clearly enough, indeed far more powerfully than if it were handed to us in the form of a lecture. We know immediately that the scullery maid's life is hard and humiliating – but also that she possesses, unnoticed by most of those around her, an exceptionally elevated and noble soul. Through Chardin's eyes, we come to know her as an aristocrat of the spirit – worthy of careful attention and admiration.

An ideology can be said to have achieved true victory when we forget it even exists. We can tell that Christianity has been one of the most powerful movements of ideas there has ever been, in part because of how seldom we notice that it has ever had the slightest influence on us.

Rembrandt van Rijn, *The Supper at Emmaus*, 1648

2

One of the most emblematic stories of Christianity is to be found towards the end of the Gospel of St Luke. Jesus has been crucified and a deep sadness has descended on his followers. Two of them are walking towards the village of Emmaus, near Jerusalem, when they are accosted by an unknown traveller. He walks with them for a while and they talk, largely about the tragic end of their beloved preacher from Galilee. When they reach Emmaus, the stranger says goodbye, but the men insist that, as it's getting late, he should interrupt his journey and stay with them for supper. As they sit down to eat and the stranger breaks bread, the two men suddenly realise, to their terror and astonishment, who is in their midst: the stranger is the risen Christ. They are in the presence of the king of kings, holy of holies, dressed in the unassuming garb of an ordinary man whom they had dismissed as another random traveller.

The theme of divinity in disguise keeps recurring in the New Testament. Jesus repeatedly encounters people who accept that there might be a Messiah, but who have such particular and rigid ideas of how this figure might look and sound that they are blinded to his presence and his message. They expect him to have certain obvious marks of elevated status. They expect him to wear a golden cloak and have a jewel-encrusted crown; a sacred light should illuminate his path; he should be able to move mountains. Yet Jesus keeps frustrating any such phantasmagorical expectations. He looks normal, he has no money, he wears cheap clothes, he is coy about performing miracles.

The essential target is snobbery, defined as a rigid preconception about where greatness and goodness, kindness and value might lie. The people Jesus meets can't disentangle appearance from reality. They can't imagine that someone might be noble but have a small income; might be intelligent but lack an education; might be rare and elevated but lack recognition and prestige.

The problem of snobbery goes way beyond the biblical context. We are, most of us, painfully like the two men on the road to Emmaus. We, too, have some unfortunately fixed ideas about what special and good people should look and sound like – and therefore constantly fail to recognise who is in our midst. Our preconceptions of nobility make us miss greatness of heart in the unassuming cloak in which it is typically dressed. We can't imagine that someone in our vicinity might have an exceptional soul – or have said and felt rare and important things.

We aren't guilty of cruelty so much as a lack of imagination. The message of St Luke's gospel should continue to provoke us because of how often we fail correctly to assess whom we have met – or in what unusual or unfamiliar guise we might find our answers.

Albrecht Dürer, *Adam* and *Eve*,
both 1507

3

Christianity proposes a dark, apparently punitive thesis about our beginnings that may nevertheless – once we consider it from the right angle – offer us a route to renewed compassion and kindness.

As related to us by the greatest theologian of antiquity, St Augustine, the Garden of Eden lacked for nothing. God gave Adam and Eve every possible advantage, he showed them only love and concern, and yet still there was something in their natures that compelled them to turn against their best interests and act darkly and mistrustfully. There was – so the suggestion runs – an inherently corrupt bias in our early ancestors: a primary lack of faith, a tendency to misunderstand situations, to reason illogically, to behave with unnecessary aggression and guile. Augustine called it 'original sin' (in Latin, *peccatum originale*). But this 'original sin' did not belong to Adam and Eve alone; it was transmitted down the generations to all of their successors. Without our having done anything in particular, we too are the heirs to a nature that isn't ever going to be straightforward or complete. There is something significantly wrong with us all. We may at points be capable of grace; we can never quite shake off tendencies to corruption.

Why would it be helpful to keep this in mind? Because once we accept the bleak verdict, we are spared the risks of misplaced expectations. To know that everyone we encounter will, at some level, be flawed reduces our fury and our disappointment with this or that problematic aspect of their characters. We can calmly accept that we aren't dealing with anyone exceptionally 'bad'; we're simply up against a side of human nature that has been difficult since our expulsion from the Garden of Eden. Christian pessimism saves us from the torture and rage of excessive hope. We have no option but to live among, and learn to forgive, our fellow broken creatures.

At the same time, the idea of original sin bids us to keep in mind the extent to which we, too, are necessarily imperfect and so renders us less embarrassed and defensive about admitting as much at speed. We get things wrong; we misjudge situations; we are constantly drawn towards unhelpful beliefs and desires. Knowing this about ourselves, we can apologise to all who have to deal with us with sincerity way ahead of time. We can laugh heartily and modestly at our short-sightedness and idiocy. Accepting that we are 'sinners' spurs us on to do better. People who believe themselves to be very good are rarely so; a keen sense of our bad tendencies provides us with heightened protection against them.

We don't need to believe in the literal story of Genesis to derive benefit from its moral. There is nothing as insufferable or as dangerous as people who hold themselves to be 'pure'. Growing at ease with the peculiar idea that we are 'sinners' readies us for the imperfect lives we are fated to lead – while bolstering our capacities for compassion and love.

Gentile Bellini, *Procession of the True Cross (Procession of the brotherhood of San Giovanni Evangelista with the true cross relic on Saint Mark's day on the Piazza San Marco)*, 1496

4

For a religion that was deeply interested in people becoming 'good', Christianity spent a lot of time warning us against the dangers of thinking that one might at any stage actually have become so.

In the religion's early days, many of those who took the New Testament seriously grew to think of themselves as an elect group. They felt that they had been chosen by God to bring about his mission for the world – and laid claim to unusual degrees of decency and virtue, integrity and honour. They were not like the infidels who had turned away from the message of salvation. Some people were going to end up in Paradise, while others would burn for eternity in the fires of Hell – and it was evident who would endure what fate. This in turn generated a rush to try to become identified as Christian by publicly converting, joining a church and leading an overtly Christian life.

The feeling that it might be a relatively simple matter to know who was 'elect', as well as to believe that one had become so, alarmed and offended the deeply pious and wise St Augustine. Being properly good and honourable was never, Augustine thought, an easy matter, something that one could settle once and for all by being baptised or memorising a few passages of the gospels; it would have to be a daily, never-completed effort.

Likewise, it was impossible for ordinary humans to set about judging who among their acquaintances might be good or bad, for they could never see deeply enough into themselves or others to make such a call. The ranks of the pure and the impure were inherently mixed as far as our faculties could discern. Augustine proposed a metaphor of two populations, what he called two cities, the city of God and the city of men. Eventually, on the Day of Judgement, these two cities would be properly populated, with the city of God filled only with the righteous and the good, and the city of men filled only with sinners and reprobates. But – crucially – this sifting was not for us to initiate right now. This would solely be something for God and his angels to carry out at a point outside of history. During our lifetimes, we could not know who might belong to what 'city'. Someone could be a beggar and have been involved in petty crimes and still, deep down, be a true invisible future citizen of the city of God. And someone else might be ostensibly decent, do good works and have charitable deeds to their name, and yet for all that, in their essence, have something gnarled and vainglorious about them that rendered them ultimately fit only for the city of men.

Augustine's point is that we can't – or should not – ourselves form any opinion about who belongs where. In a sideswipe at the organised religion of his own time, Augustine proposed that even the church was not to be thought of as inhabited only or simply by godly people. It wasn't because a person wore a bishop's cope that they could be guaranteed to have an ethical soul or because they were a prostitute that they were a lost cause.

We were being warned – once again – against the dangers of righteousness and easy judgement. We can't tell who belongs where in the hierarchy of goodness; this is a task of which only a supernatural being would be capable. And therefore, our duty on this Earth is simple: to be kind and imaginative about whomever crosses our path, and continuously on our guard against any belief in our own preordained nobility.

Hubert and Jan van Eyck, *The Virgin Mary*, detail from the Ghent Altarpiece, 1423–1432

5.

An area where the modern secular realm and the Christian past appear to agree wholeheartedly is on the subject of love: both are united in deeming it the most important dynamic in the world. It is because of this seeming unity that we are apt to miss just how distinctive, and how rewardingly unusual, the Christian approach to love really is.

We tend to understand love as a response to perfection and strength in another human. Our sense of love is elicited by, and grows stronger in relation to, beauty, intelligence and accomplishment. When explaining why we love someone, we might want to point to their exceptional wit or cleverness, their social confidence or the sheen of their eyes.

What would be very unusual is to stress that we loved someone because of their weakness, their incapacity, their brokenness; to say that we loved them because the world found them unimpressive, because they had a bad reputation, many difficult sides to their characters and plenty that needed to be excused. However, these are precisely the targets of Christian love, a love that is drawn to whatever in us is lacking and in need of redemption, a love that extends imagination and sympathy towards whomever is suffering and lost, dejected and forlorn.

In this respect, Christian love is closer to its parental than its romantic counterpart: parents may feel pleased for their child when they are thriving and popular at school. They are likely to feel particular tenderness and care, though, when this child is in a mess: sick and unable to cope, confused and lonely, needing to sit on a parent's lap and have their brow gently stroked as the tears fall.

As a consequence of this focus on our vulnerability, Christian love is especially melancholy in temper and appearance. Secular modern love might celebrate the proud and joyful moments. Christian love is on hand when the darkness closes in.

It is no coincidence that the central fount of love in the Christian story, the Virgin Mary, should so often be depicted as serious, concerned and sorrowful. She is both the most loving figure in the gospels and the most melancholy in spirit. She has room for our pain. She understands that we are not able, or meant, to triumph all the time, that we are inherently fragile and in need of assistance, that even though we may be adults, much in us retains the needs of childhood, that we might crave to be taken in someone's arms and be told not much else other than, 'I understand ...'

Christianity helpfully reminds us that our deepest wish in love isn't so much to celebrate and triumph with someone as to cry quietly with them.

Courtly love, depicted in the
Codex Manesse, an anthology of
poetry, Zurich, c. 1300–1340

6

Christianity has so often been hastily depicted as a religion of prudes, prigs and moralistic virgins that we should dare to explore in greater depth and with greater sympathy why – in certain modes – it has chosen to place such emphasis on the non-sexual aspects of love.

One of the high points of this tendency came about at the end of the 11th century in the aristocratic circles of Europe. Under the aegis of Christianity, in the royal courts of Provence, ducal Burgundy, Champagne and Aquitaine, it was newly imagined that the point of love might not be so much about sex as about friendship; the apotheosis of love was pictured as a sympathy of souls rather than a passionate intercourse of bodies. In the songs and poetry of the genre that the French came to know as *l'amour courtois* (courtly or, more accurately, courteous or polite love), figures like Bernart de Ventadorn, Giraut de Bornelh and the Duke of Aquitaine made a case for relationships in which energy normally channelled into physical passion would be redirected towards conversation, kindness and psychological exploration. This was not a case being put forward by people lacking the confidence or attributes to form a more standard relationship. It was a reasoned conclusion by aristocratic knights and courtiers who, having tasted many different kinds of living arrangements, had come to feel that pleasure and interest might lie more in friendship than in an affair or a marriage. Two people properly in love should – according to this vision – never take each other for granted; they should talk at length of their feelings and pay inordinate attention to their mutual requirements and sorrows. They were to be the best and deepest sort of friends.

The troubadours were rediscovering a key distinction in the vocabulary of love used by the ancient Greeks: a distinction between love as *eros* (desire) and love as *agape* (tenderness or sympathy). And they were, in a spirit that remains revolutionary and provocative to this day, urging us to focus on the advantages of the latter over those of the former.

We are prone to thinking that if someone we feel ready to love proposes friendship rather than eroticism, we have been short-changed and humiliated. What should give us new perspective and (at points) hope is a clearer awareness of just how much kindness, tolerance and curiosity so-called mere friends can offer one another, as opposed to the possessiveness, jealousy and desire to control that dominate a great many relationships. The apparent consolation prize may in truth be the real attainment.

Christianity nudges us to imagine that what we are really seeking in love – sympathy, supportiveness and a sense of respect – may be easiest to locate in a figure that our age has curiously and unfairly downgraded and maligned: the friend.

Fra Angelico, *Noli Me Tangere*,
c. 1442. Fresco in the Church and
convent of San Marco, Florence, Italy

7

Christianity introduces us with particular clarity to an unusual idea that the modern secular world has long resisted, at great cost to its own development: that reading a book cannot possibly – or for long – change anyone's thoughts or behaviour.

It is common to assume that the best chances of developing our minds must lie in trying to nourish ourselves with concepts found in great literary and philosophical works. In spite of its reverence for books, Christianity never trusted in such high-minded, windy optimism. It knew us to be far more forgetful and flighty creatures than this. It took us to be people who would, under practical pressure, reliably overlook everything they knew: the ideas they were committed to, the vows they had made, the values they cherished.

For this reason, Christianity never settled on merely being an extended book club or lending library; it understood that it needed to become a gigantic machine for rehearsing and enforcing ideas. At great cost and with an admirable command of logistics and finance, therefore, it set up material structures that could support and bolster its theories. It asked us to repeat lessons on a life-long basis. Up to eight times a day, it asked us to get on our knees and say the very same things, because it knew that what was clear and convincing at 6 a.m. could grow rusty by midday (unlike the modern education system that blithely assumes it will be enough to deliver a set of ideas dryly once or twice in a school room). It asked us to memorise texts, it pioneered ways of enthralling audiences through rhetoric, it inscribed dates in our diaries, it ringed off periods throughout the year when we had to pay special attention to specific concepts and it told us stories of exceptional people who put the Christian philosophy to work in their own lives. It recognised that we will always be creatures of the senses, not just of reason, and hence it tried to reach us through music, food, incantation, sculpture, painting, smell and light. It hired the finest artists, architects, designers and musicians of every age, appreciating that we would need the help of Bach's Mass in B Minor, the rose window of Chartres Cathedral and Giotto's wall paintings to keep the ideas we theoretically assented to active in our minds.

One of the greatest innovations within this omnipresent, multisensory approach to teaching was the development of the monastery. Christianity proposed that some of us might need to put ourselves behind high walls and live among a group of like-minded people in an environment of particular beauty and solemnity. We might need to throw away our distractions and sleep night after night in calm and uplifting bedrooms like those designed by the architect Michelozzo di Bartolomeo (1396–1472) and painted by the Dominican brother Fra Angelico (c. 1395–1455) in Florence in the convent of San Marco in the 15th century.

We have been too hopeful about ourselves. We will never evolve internally so long as we keep using our phones and limit ourselves to the odd book (or holiday abroad, chat with a friend or session with a therapist). The success of Christianity should alert us to the fact that, if our goal is the reformation of the spirit, we are going to need a lot more: architecture, music, silence, self-censorship, food, ritual, a calendar, a community, pilgrimages and – most complicatedly of all – monasteries. We may have plenty of good ideas (and fantastic dreams). But they'll remain exactly that until we understand – with Christianity's help – what careless and inattentive creatures we really are, and therefore the scale of the practical and aesthetic structures we are going to need to build to become who we really want to be.

Anonymous architect, façade of
Strasbourg Cathedral ('Plan A1'),
Strasbourg, France, 1260s

8

Given the way most cities look (aggressive, chaotic, terrifying), it's unfortunate how much we rely on the quality of our buildings to keep our minds afloat and balanced. We may even forget the extent to which the challenging architecture all around us is quietly destroying our spirits until, every now and then, we stumble upon a building so impeccable and refined that it ends up making us very sad – as extreme beauty sometimes can.

In the European Middle Ages, Christianity was responsible for putting up some of the finest ecclesiastical buildings ever known. Looking around the cathedrals of Wells or Amiens, Rouen or Strasbourg today, we may end up not just impressed, but also tearful – because of how these symbols of tenderness and care, courage and vision stand out amidst the mediocrity of ordinary life.

We may never have built more than a sandcastle, but we can still understand – semiconsciously – how buildings stand and the moves required to make them do so in particular ways. We understand, for example, that fluted columns require a great deal more work than plain cylindrical ones, that rose windows containing thousands of bits of coloured glass are a work of patient genius, that to carve angels on a ceiling 150 metres above the ground is no ordinary feat and that to chisel stone until it resembles the folds of linen brushes up against the limits of the laws of physics. In other words, if we can put it like this, we understand that great cathedrals are works of love.

When someone loves properly, they go beyond what is ordinarily required. A parent with a child, a lover with their intimate will pay attention to the most minor details; they will put in a degree of patience and perseverance that can never be demanded or legislated for. They will give freely from a pure wish to assist – and because they are not 'keeping score'.

There is something of this boundless love in Christian Gothic architecture. In the domain of stone and glass, of arches and tracery, we locate some of the same qualities as animate the highest kinds of human relationships. We know what would have been needed simply to shelter us – and appreciate how much further these builders went, without the help of a single mechanical tool.

If we feel sad under the cathedral roof, it's because our own lives are by comparison so hard and cold. Perhaps when we were younger, the impact would have been less powerful. The more difficulties we have gone through, the more the tenderness and devotion on display risk touching us. We might wish that the thoughtfulness and concern that went into the mullions and quatrefoils could have more of a role in our bedrooms and offices. We realise that we are more tired and lonely than we knew.

Christianity may still, paradoxically, leave us uninclined to believe; but no matter. The sense of being moved by its architecture is telling us something key: that we, too, harbour profound longings for harmony, gentleness and love – and that, without guiding us towards any particular doctrine, the cathedrals have given us something to live up to and hope for.

V.
Hinduism

An eight-spoked wheel decorating the
Hindu Konark Sun Temple in India,
13th century CE

1

Hinduism is both salutary and original in proposing that there is nothing especially noble or interesting about being alive. Once we look at matters dispassionately, a lot of what we have to go through is misery and suffering: we need – with great effort – to grow up, to assume responsibilities, to master a profession, to have a family, to take our place in societies full of backbiting and hypocrisy, to watch those we love get ill and eventually to succumb to old age ourselves. To think highly of 'life' is, through a Hindu lens, a fundamental intellectual error.

As Hinduism sees it, our real purpose is to be done with life forever; that is the true summit of existence. Hinduism reverses the Western equation: the sinful and blinkered are forced to live forever, but the righteous and awakened are privileged enough to be able to die. If we are not careful, if we do not show sufficient mercy and imagination toward others, we may well – Hinduism suggests – be subjected to the ultimate punishment: we will have to carry on into eternity.

The symbol of this ghastly on-goingness is the eight-spoked wheel of *samsara*, the most commonly depicted item in the religion, which evokes the pitiless and unceasing nature of life – to which we are committed unless we take a disciplined series of averting actions that together comprise the central components of Hindu ethics.

Hinduism does not suggest that we will carry on forever in our own bodies. According to the process of *samsara*, we are reborn into a succession of different outward envelopes, as each example is eroded away and disintegrated by time. Because *samsara* is at work across the whole animal kingdom, we might find that our enduring soul (*atman*) transmigrates at our death into the body of a woodlouse, a pelican or a house spider (though we might also be reborn as a paediatric nurse or the president). What determines the quality of the migration is the degree of *karma*, or virtue, that we have accrued in our lives. Among the many reasons why we might have to be kind to others is an awareness that unkindness might wind up with our suffering a cycle or two of life as a cockroach or a naked mole rat.

Along the way, Hinduism generates an uncommon degree of respect and tenderness for all living things. When we look at a wasp or crab, we aren't contemplating creatures fundamentally different from ourselves; their *atman* might, a few turns of the wheel of life ago, have been located in a High Court judge or a dental hygienist. We might, as a result – as most Hindus do – feel it appropriate to stick to a vegetarian diet, lest one unwittingly eat one's old uncle or geography teacher.

The suspicion that life is constantly painful and anxious is one that we largely have to bear in a very lonely way in the philosophies of the West; in those of the East, pessimism is ennobled and takes centre stage. We are permitted to feel weary and amply dissatisfied; we have, without quite knowing it, been alive since the start of creation – and it is untenably exhausting and frustrating. The trick, and the true prize, will be to be good and wise enough to learn to achieve a peaceful final end.

Fazal Sheikh, *Dawn along the Yamuna*
River, Vrindavan, India, 2003

2

For Hindus, the way to step off the treadmill of eternal existence relies – first and foremost – on a piece of intellectual insight. We cease to be subject to *samsara* and are delivered into the comforting repose of the ultimate reality known as *brahman* once we realise that, despite many appearances to the contrary, however paradoxical or absurd the idea might sound, we and the universe are in truth one.

From the earliest age, we tend to assume the very opposite. It seems self-evident that we are one kind of thing and the tree over there, the relative over here, the clouds in the sky, the monkey on the parapet and the river wending its way to the sea belong to quite different categories. Yet Hinduism insists that our belief in difference belongs ultimately to a realm of *maya* or illusion. If we look more deeply into the nature of things, through the help of teaching and spiritual exercises, we stand to discover the remarkable unity of all elements. Unlike what appearances imply, everything we can see and experience around us belongs to the same life force: the leaves unfurling on the tree, the child learning to read, the earthworm digging its tunnels and the lava bubbling from the earth, all belong to a single unitary power, which only egoistic prejudice has hitherto prevented us from acknowledging as one.

Most of our pain, Hinduism argues, arises from an over-eager attachment to the difference between ourselves and the rest of the world. We pay inordinate attention to who has slightly more money or respect than we do, and we are constantly humiliated by people and events that don't seem to honour our sense of uniqueness.

In a process known as *moksha* or liberation, we can throw off the veil of illusion that works to separate us from the universe and can start to identify with cosmic totality. It no longer matters exactly where we end and others begin; everything belongs to the same whole that we have mistakenly and unnecessarily carved up into parts. There is a little less reason to grasp, to be puffed up, to be proud or to become embittered. We can survey the course of our lives and of our societies with calm indifference. We can cease to identify happiness with the working out of our will upon the world – and take in with compassion and serenity whatever destiny throws our way. We enjoy *paripurna-brahmanubhava*, the experience of oneness with brahman, the principle of all things.

Once we have let go of our own ego like this, we may have a few more years left to live, but we can be sure that – eventually – we will not need to keep returning. Constant rebirth is the fate of those who cleave too tightly to their own selves. By contrast, those who have learnt to surrender can at their demise merge with the universe and will never need to suffer the indignities of individual life again.

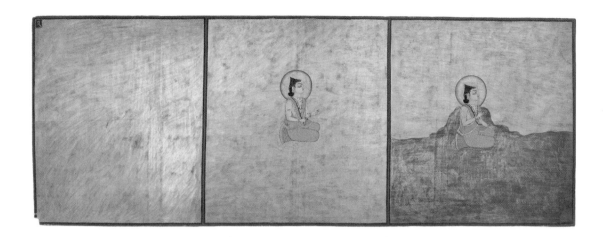

Three aspects of the Absolute, from
a manuscript of the *Nath Charit*
(attributed to Bulaki), 1823

3

On the right-hand side of the triptych, a figure is seated on the ground, practising yoga. The Sanskrit word *yoga* means 'yoking' and refers to the way in which the discipline allows us – through meditation, a range of postures and rules for breathing – to tame the runaway mind and body, so that we can overcome the ego and its passions and contemplate the cosmos with serenity. In the central image, such is the yogi's spiritual progress, the ground has disappeared from under his legs. By the last image, the yogi has disappeared altogether: he has managed to forget himself, his mind has merged with the universe, he has become a part of the absolute.

Central to the wisdom of Hinduism is its intense devotion to trying to find ways to manage the varied agonies of being human. The wise person isn't so much someone who has removed difficulties from their life – one can only ever make so much progress in this direction – as someone who has found techniques for alleviating whatever distress comes their way. Hinduism gives us a word, *titiksha*, to describe the noble art of enduring suffering.

Someone who has become adept at *titiksha* does not expect things to go well: an advanced degree of pessimism is a bedrock of Hindu wisdom. Our aim should be to nurture a capacity for indifference based on an awareness of the nullity of all of life's apparent prizes. The devotee of *titiksha* begins by practising on relatively small issues: typically, they might try to strengthen their disregard for heat and cold. They might spend a chilly night outdoors and some uncomfortable periods in the noonday sun. They might then learn to endure great boredom – spending hours in a small blank room with nothing to keep them from their own thoughts – and follow this up by honing their powers of concentration at the centre of a noisy marketplace. From there, they might strengthen their indifference to reputation. They might say something provocative (but true) to a group of prejudiced people and develop their ability not to be ruffled by the clamour that ensues. They might equally well train at remaining immune to praise and flattery, noticing and undermining the pull of their own vanity. The opinions of almost everyone simply should not matter. After years of exercise, they would hope to find themselves substantially immune to the vagaries of health, success, esteem and love.

We are used to the idea of exercise in relation to the body. We know that we cannot hope to be physically fit without a lot of practice, but we resist comparable moves in relation to our minds. Here, we imagine that one or two wise ideas will settle immediately in our consciousness and determine our thoughts for the long term. Hinduism more sensibly sets us to work. The West has come to know yoga as principally a physical activity; but in its pure Hindu form it is a set of psycho-spiritual exercises skilfully designed to release the mind from its corrupt attachments.

We aren't looking to have more supple bodies (though this cannot hurt); we should strain ourselves to achieve the sort of mind that can forget the very ground we sit on.

Ravi Varma Press, *Lakshmi*, 1894

4

We might expect that a religion devoted to spiritual enlightenment would have scant concern for money and possessions. But Hinduism surprises and challenges us by suggesting that – despite everything – what it calls *artha,* or a concern for material prosperity, has a place within a wise life.

Hinduism is not directing us towards crass materialism. It doesn't want to exhaust us with overly rich foods or attention-seeking displays of wealth. It is aware – with a touching practicality – that many good and elevated things require a degree of financial support in order to go well. We won't be able to undertake spiritual exercises unless we can take a considerable amount of time off from practical duties every day. Meditation on nothingness can be substantially assisted by having a servant or two to take care of the laundry and the housekeeping. We need to have enough money for books – and for a home whose decoration is in line with our values. Friendships and relationships can be enhanced rather than destroyed by well-deployed wealth. What Hinduism calls *metta*, or loving kindness, thrives on enough money to buy presents, clothes, food and shelter for those one cares for.

Though it has its ascetic sides, Hinduism does not make the error (which so bedevils Christianity) of assuming that poverty is a prerequisite of purity and goodness. It knows that poor people have to think about money a lot more often and deeply than prosperous ones: the point of having money is not to feel proud or enamoured of it, but to be able to stop thinking about it altogether.

Hindus traditionally direct their hopes for material comfort to Lakshmi, the goddess of prosperity. One of the most popular of all Hindu deities, she is typically represented holding two lotus flowers that speak of spiritual liberation as well as material good fortune. She is usually accompanied by at least one elephant, a symbol of power and strength, and a swan, an animal that is at home both in the air and in the water, and thereby speaks of an ability to combine competence in the material and spiritual realms.

Lakshmi understands, and would never condemn, our appetite for a better house or a higher-paying job. Her role isn't to make us feel guilty about wanting more wealth, but to remind us that the true point of money is – in the end – to enable us to forget about money.

Yashoda with the Infant
Krishna, India, Chola period,
early 12th century

5.

Most world religions and philosophies make the cardinal error of supposing that what they believe to be the meaning of life should – by virtue of its importance – apply to everyone, irrespective of age, circumstance or position. So proud are they of their insight into existence, they can't help but accord it universal and dogmatic application.

Hinduism is a great deal more supple and imaginative. It, too, has a sense of how a good life should be lived but, crucially, it never assumes that the rules should apply across the board. It cuts up populations into segments – and differentiates right conduct according to four life stages collectively called *ashramas*. The first of these *ashramas* is termed *brahmacharya* and covers childhood and studenthood. Here – however serious life might be overall – the individual is allowed to play, to be tender and to give free rein to the imagination, though they must also learn and obey. Then, more arduously, comes the stage when a person becomes a *grihastha* or householder: this is the time for maximal involvement in practical matters. There might be little time for prayer or contemplation; it's the moment for building up capital, for buying a house, developing a profession and having a family of one's own. The stage might last twenty years or more. Eventually, practical obligations recede, children grow up and leave home and it is time to become a *vanaprastha* or 'forest walker': someone who can increasingly surrender practical tasks and reorient themselves to the spiritual realm by going for walks – ideally (and poetically) in mango forests. Then, lastly, when we are truly done with business and when family life has ceased to make all but the most minor calls on us, we are allowed to enter the stage of *sannyasa*, in which we renounce worldly goods, don a simple robe and wander the world in search of ultimate sources of enlightenment, charity and spiritual friendship.

We may not agree with every detail of the way Hinduism carves up a life, but we can admire the imaginative way in which it seeks to align its teachings with the particular demands of society, the body and the family across time. It would – knows Hinduism – be as absurd to entice an 18-year-old to do yoga for six hours a day while contemplating the absolute as it would be to spend all one's time in business meetings as a 70-year-old. There is a time for *moksha*, the striving to liberate oneself from the cycle of eternal life, and there is a time for *artha*, when we must head to the office and sound serious during company presentations. Both are, in their respective contexts, equally legitimate and equally important.

We are reminded that there is no simplistic unitary goal to life. We shouldn't ask ourselves what the right way to live is, per se; it all depends on where on the journey we happen to be.

Loving couple (*mithuna*), temple
carving, Orissa, India, Eastern
Ganga dynasty, 13th century

We have come to expect very little by way of encouragement or sympathy in relation to sex from religions. At best, a blind eye; at worst, a constant hounding and reminder of the evils of the flesh.

Hinduism surprises us by not only tolerating sex, but also by connecting it to the highest values and the ultimate ends of life. Nothing shocked the British more, when they reached northern India in the 18th century, than to find temples of exquisite architectural refinement covered, in certain sections, with graphic sculptures of figures engaged in anal play, threesomes, oral sex, bondage and foot fetishism. They at first imagined that these might have been add-ons perpetrated by a degenerate cult or invading foreign tribe; only gradually did it become clear that Hinduism – for all its highflown concerns – was underpinned by a hugely ambitious sense of the role and pleasures of the body.

The religion made the remarkable step of placing sexual fulfilment – *kama* – among the four puruṣārthas, or aims of human life, alongside *dharma* (morality), *artha* (prosperity) and *moksha* (spiritual liberation). It implicitly deemed a successful orgasm as the equal of ethical conduct or devotional education. Hinduism's respect for sex was rooted in a particular understanding of what lies behind our erotic feelings. These do not stem – as has so often been alleged – from a base animal impulse; they are a means by which we can sense the unity of the universe (*brahman*).

Normally, we live beneath a veil of illusion, which persuades us of the separateness of all things, bodies included, but our sexual desires push us to break down the barriers between ourselves and others. This explains Hinduism's particular interest in explicit practices. The more extreme things become, the more vigorously and directly we are able to transcend the self. With a partner we love, in an atmosphere of safety and trust, we can take another's sexual organs into our mouth, or explore their anus with our toes – and thereby bridge the alienation that normally and unnecessarily prevails between human beings. We might colloquially say that we are turned on, but through a Hindu lens, at the core of our excitement is the sense that we are breaking down the illusion of separateness and taking a small but important step towards oneness with what we can, without exaggeration, following the religion, term the universe. We may, at a material level, simply have our fingers deep inside another's most private folds; spiritually, we are opening ourselves up to cosmic totality.

Almost all religions have refused to pick up on the deeper themes that run through our physical longings. Hinduism had the intelligence and imagination to understand that what is in the end exciting about sex is not the mere rubbing of organs, but the promise of an end to metaphysical loneliness.

VI.
Buddhism

Taidō Shūfū, *Ensō*, 19th century

It may feel a little exaggerated to claim that one could fall in love with an entire culture and religion because of its habit of drawing circles on bits of paper. But the closer we come to Zen Buddhist Japan and its tradition of the *ensō*, the more we might conclude that such an emotion would not be out of place.

The making of *ensō* (circular) drawings began in Japan in the 9th century. They may look like 'art', but, like most Buddhist cultural creations, they are in reality tools for psycho-spiritual development. Buddhism has no concept of art existing for its own sake; it is a practical, therapeutic practice designed to help us attain a state of calm, gratitude, wonder and fearlessness. It is an extension of philosophy and its goal is our enlightenment.

According to Zen Buddhism, the chief source of our agitation stems from not being able to set ourselves and our challenges into their true and wider contexts. We are prone to stand far too close to our concerns and to exaggerate the scale of our ego and our importance in the whole. This is not merely vainglorious, it is also needlessly painful; we read insult where none was meant, we exhaust ourselves trying to stand out, we suffer from a mixture of misplaced pride and an equally misplaced sense of humiliation.

Buddhism keeps trying – through a variety of means – to draw us back to a universal perspective; the *ensō* comprises one more such manoeuvre. In a mood of agitation, a Zen practitioner is advised to find a quiet space, a large sheet of washi (thin Japanese paper) and an ink brush – and then, in either one or two strokes, to complete a circle, with the aim of directing their mind back to the totality. Many *ensō*s are accompanied by small philosophical poems or aphorisms. This one, by the Japanese nun and teacher Ryōnen Gensō (1646–1711), tells us characteristically:

> When you understand yourself fully,
> There is no single thing.

In other words, in our moments of enlightened consciousness, we can overcome our obsession with our own 'I'. We can see ourselves within the true circle of existence and time, and therefore don't need to lament our condition, the brevity of our life, the paucity of our achievements and the number of our flaws.

An *ensō* on our wall will help to guard our equilibrium. In the midst of agitation, we will be able to throw a glance at the simple, bold brushstroke and recover our sense of the redemptively negligible place that we and our troubles occupy in the vastness of the universe.

Sengai Gibon, Copy of *The Universe*,
Japan, 18th century

2.

Zen Buddhism has, throughout its history, expressed itself first and foremost in a minimalist way. Its guiding principle has been that we need to hear things expressed very simply and very clearly. It knows that we are assaulted day to day by a plethora of stimuli that worry our spirits and prevent us from deepening our relationship to the concepts on which our sanity and balance rely. The task of the philosopher-artist is therefore – as much as possible – to empty the sensory plane and quieten our inputs, so that what is true and necessary can assume its proper importance in our injured minds.

The Western complaint that there might not be 'enough' in a picture to merit attention (or respect), and the attendant association between so-called masterpieces and busy-ness and technical complication, make no sense within the Zen Buddhist canon. What can it matter if a poem is made up of only a few lines built out of the most ordinary and homespun words, or if a picture has just three geometric shapes to its name? 'Greatness' in art isn't related to encyclopaedic knowledge or technical gymnastics; it is the consequence of pointing a viewer with graceful modesty and restraint to what is essential but always in danger of being submerged in the chaos of everyday life. And the task of the viewer isn't to seek hidden meanings or esoteric references, but to look the simple truth in the eye and let it – as it may not have done in a long time – resonate properly in their heart.

Perhaps the most moving example of this form of minimal Zen Buddhist art was completed by the monk and thinker Sengai Gibon (1750–1838) in the early 18th century; the image is, to the Japanese, as well known and revered as the *Mona Lisa* is to Westerners. The title makes its intention clear: this ostensibly simple drawing is about nothing less than 'everything'. It is – in a highly compressed form – a guide to life.

The square represents the Four Noble Truths of Buddhism: firstly, that we must understand that all existence involves suffering and anguish. Secondly, that the cause of this suffering lies in the mind's constant craving for perfection and accumulation. Thirdly, that suffering can end when we bring our craving under control. And fourthly, that Buddhism directs us to a path by which we can overcome our pain.

In Sengai Gibon's image, the square is linked to a triangle that represents the self – which is in turn connected to the circle, emblem of totality, perspective and wisdom. Once we connect ourselves to Buddhism's truths, the image tells us, we will achieve the enlightenment and serenity we have longed for from the start.

It took the West around a thousand years longer than Japan to understand what minimalism can offer us: a concentrated dose of truth and calm, shorn of everything extraneous, lifted above the clamour of ordinary life. We are used to dismissing certain works of art by saying that 'a child could have made them'. Zen Buddhism's answer would be that it might take a whole lifetime to grasp the full import of what Sengai Gibon's three ostensibly simple shapes have to tell us.

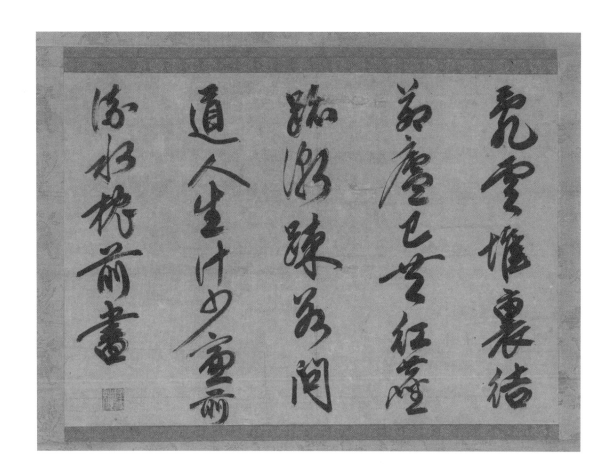

Sesson Yūbai, *Poem on the Theme of a Monk's Life*, Japan, first half of the 14th century

3

In spite of the West's immense reverence for language, the region has been slow to imagine that the act of handwriting might constitute an art form in itself. We are used to honouring words principally for what they have to tell us, not for how they appear on a page. The East has been more imaginative in proposing that, in the hands of a talented practitioner, a script might well deserve all the consideration that we would be prepared to accord to a portrait or landscape painting. It has argued that the way someone writes a piece of text might play a central role in ensuring that its ideas can be heard with suitable sonority and depth.

Sesson Yūbai (1290–1347) was a 14th-century Zen Buddhist monk, poet and calligrapher who spent twenty-three years in China learning the art of writing. He was especially acclaimed for the vigour of his brushstrokes and his emphasis on the diagonals of his characters. Most of his poems speak – as so much of Buddhism does – of the importance and value of a simple, unshowy life. In this example, he writes:

```
My thatched hut is woven with
disordered layers of clouds.
Already my footprints are washed
away with the red dust.
If you ask, this monk has few
plans for his life:
Before my window, flowing waters;
facing my pillow, books.
```

There is often a sense, when we see someone's handwriting for the first time, that we understand them in a new and more intimate way. We may have exchanged texts and emails with them for years, but when we see the nuances of their writing, their words take on a fresh poignancy: their tenderness comes more clearly into focus, we can sympathise with their underlying anxieties, and the effort that they put into the business of living (as implied by the careful curls of their letters) is more starkly in evidence. We might not expect the handwritten version of Sesson Yūbai's poem to tell us anything very different from the printed one, but the distinction – albeit quiet – is immense: in the latter, we hear what he says, in the former, we seem to hear who he is.

Handwriting does not only benefit the viewer. The increased effort of writing out words by hand also helps their meaning to sink more deeply into our minds as authors. In order that certain valuable ideas can assume the role we want them to play in our lives, Buddhism advises us to write them out carefully in our own script – repeatedly, over many years.

It would be an immense disservice merely to call the Buddhist calligraphic tradition quaint or historically interesting. We should be practical enough to think of stealing its relevant parts and putting these to work in our own psychological lives.

Muqi Fachang, *Six Persimmons*, China,
Southern Song dynasty, 13th century

4.

Everything has become abundant; everything is in reach; we can have produce from the four corners. Fruit is flown in from anywhere – even persimmons, that taste rich and honey-like when ripe and have the texture of an apricot and a skin like an apple's.

The tragedy is that we don't notice anything much of what we have. Buddhism takes aim at our haste and our neglect. In failing to appreciate the things before us, we become far more avaricious and dissatisfied than we need to be. We dream of fame and elevated status. We call our circumstances narrow and uninspiring; in reality, we have omitted remotely to pay them justice. We seek a better world, without having taken stock of the one already to hand. If we were able to open our eyes, there would be so many universes for us to see right in front of us.

The Chinese Buddhist monk (one is never just an 'artist' in Buddhism) Muqi Fachang (c. 1210–1269) completed his rendition of six persimmons in the middle of the 13th century. Those with a sympathy for the lessons of his creed have been looking at them carefully ever since, especially after they reached Japan in 1606 and were given pride of place in a meditation hall in the Daitoku-ji temple in Kyoto.

There is ostensibly nothing very special about the persimmons – and that is precisely the point. Those who are in a hurry, those who are unable in the end to notice and draw value from anything, will rush past these as they will so much else. Muqi is trying to slow down our impatient gaze. He deliberately empties the visual field and sets these modest works of nature in front of us for reflective contemplation, daring us to ignore them while also beseeching us – with all the resources of his art – not to.

The painting's guardians in Kyoto traditionally asked that we pause to look at the work for at least three minutes: that can feel like an awfully long time. When we accept the challenge, after around the first thirty seconds, our breathing is likely to slow and we may start to see how much there is to appreciate. Each persimmon, though 'the same' from a distance, emerges as distinctive in size, shape and colour. What we might initially have thought of as identical declares itself as rife with difference. Each persimmon is – we can now see – as individual as a child is to its parent.

What Muqi asked us to do with pieces of fruit, we might carry out with the world more broadly: we might take a second and third look at loaves of bread, clouds, paving stones, the books on our shelves, blades of grass and – most importantly – one another. Once we have learnt to draw value from inexpensive things, we can never be poor – whatever our level of wealth – and we can never be bored, however quiet things might have become. The persimmons are, with great humility, doing momentous work for us: they are pointing us to a path of liberation.

Figure of Budai Hesheng, China,
Ming dynasty, 1486

5.

Buddhism gives off every sign of being an unremittingly pessimistic philosophy. It loses few opportunities to remind us that life is suffering, that disappointment is the rule and that we are fated to witness all our hopes and aspirations destroyed with time.

It can, therefore, feel a little paradoxical to come across the cult of Budai, a Chinese monk who became a saintly figure within Buddhism in the 10th century. He is frequently represented in statues and on wall hangings, celebrated for his laughter, quick wit and large belly, which he loved to rub while throwing back his head and chuckling warmly. What is a portly comedian doing in this religion of lamentation and sorrow? Why should we want to laugh, given what Buddhism has to tell us about our earthly prospects?

The paradox is only superficial. In essence, Buddhism wants to shake us from our pretensions, our complacency and our misplaced perfectionism – and if these are its goals, then it sees no logical reason why they might not be accomplished as much via a set of witticisms as a funereal lament.

Buddhism cannily understood that most humour is the result of being directed with special zest and energy to the omnipresent gap between our hopes and the available reality. We laugh not because things are happy, but precisely because we have been helped to recognise that they are so damnably and incorrigibly sad. Our laughter represents a release of tension at the awfulness of everything.

We might laugh darkly at a joke that tells us that going on holiday offers us a 'chance to be unhappy somewhere else with better weather …' Or one that celebrates marriage as an institution that generously offers us one specific person to blame for all our hitherto free-floating misery. Or that adolescence is a phase kindly designed by nature to ensure that we won't end up overly sad that our children are soon going to be leaving home. Laughter is an involuntary spasm provoked by a pithy, skilful assessment of the fundamental misery of existence.

Importantly, we tend to laugh in company. Humour is a social activity. Dark truths that we had contemplated alone, with embarrassment and a sense of having been persecuted by fate, are given a chance to be shared among friends. That we are all laughing together is proof that we are not – whatever our suspicions – actually alone. We are fellow suffering humans facing up to similar sources of frustration and grief. As individuals, we have not been accorded an especially unpleasant destiny. It turns out that everyone is crying – and therefore laughing – about careers, marriages, ageing, money and children.

The secular West has traditionally relegated comedy to the realm of 'entertainment'; it is 'just' for laughs. Buddhism has been more ambitious. It understood that trying to elicit laughter can be the most effective means of prompting people to confront their pain and isolation. It isn't a diversion from so-called serious things: it is the most graceful and kindly way of helping us to acknowledge and make our peace with them.

Dong Qichang, *Invitation to Reclusion
at Jingxi*, China, Ming Dynasty, 1611

6

Buddhist art has, from the outset, paid an uncommon degree of attention to lives spent in huts in the deepest countryside, in the shadow of large mountains, days away from the nearest hamlet or village. Poems have been written about, and drawings made of, the pleasures of having only the tiniest dwelling to look after, of passing the time among pine trees, of admiring flowers and birds, of eating simple food and seeing almost no one except for the odd fellow hermit or farmer.

Dong Qichang's (1555–1636) drawing of a couple of huts in a natural landscape is typical. This is the sort of place where substantial happiness can be found, Dong is telling us. We would go to sleep to the sound of the river, our peace would be undisturbed, our days devoted to philosophy and reading.

It's surprising to learn, therefore, that Dong himself was a high-ranking court official in the Ming dynasty and spent most of his life in Beijing carrying out important business for the emperor, communicating with other civil servants and attending to urgent military and economic affairs of state. Why then the huts?

Dong was not alone. Buddhism's paeans of praise to rural existence held special appeal not to peasants and retirees but to their opposites: the wealthiest, most active segments of Chinese society. The reason was that elite life was especially treacherous and exhausting. Ming politics were rife with backbiting, disloyalty and sudden reversals. At any moment, a glorious career built up carefully over decades might be extinguished on the whim of the emperor or a venal courtier.

Buddhism's celebration of the simple hut was – in the circumstances – the ultimate insurance policy. It reminded those who were taking risks and might end up losing their status that there was nothing to fear about the swerves and upsets of ambition. If they were to be sacked, they did not have to suffer unduly or eternally. There was genuine pleasure in being away from people, in the beauty of nature and the consolation of meditation and calligraphy.

We often lead lives more timid than we should because we exaggerate the downsides of ambition. We tell ourselves that we could not survive without a certain sort of income – and therefore turn down opportunities to follow our real aspirations. We are so scared of upsetting the powerful that we rein in our real thoughts – and thereby throttle our chances of making a mark.

Buddhism proposes that we have misunderstood the scale of our needs and the consequences of worldly failure. We have imagined that life would become unbearable far earlier than it truly would be. In fact, years spent in a hut could be more than adequate. There would be birdsong and healthy walks outdoors, quiet evenings and friendship with the stars. There is a role in this soothing advice for art. Buddhist thinkers didn't just tell us not to worry. They used their skill to ensure that we could feel – rather than just coldly understand – the charm of the woods.

In fact, Dong never made it to a hut. He continued to have a complicated and dynamic career in town. All the same, as a committed Buddhist, his knowledge that a hut was always there waiting for him is part of what lent him the courage and energy to risk what he needed to in order to succeed.

Gardens of Tokai-an, Kyoto, Japan,
18th century

7

Tokai-an is a Buddhist temple and monastery founded in Kyoto, Japan in 1484. Some 300 years later, it acquired three meditative rock gardens – known as *karesansui* – which its monks used to help them loosen their earthly attachments and awaken their minds to the infinite.

The first garden at Tokai-an is bare in the extreme: a field of white gravel perfectly raked into long lines. The second is made up of a bed of moss interspersed with miniature trees and a pond. And the last contains seven stones set among concentric circles of special *shirakawa-suna* gravel from the nearby Shirakawa River, famed for its muted tone achieved through a judicious admixture of black and grey sand. All these gardens are *tsuboniwa*, small spaces lined with elevated platforms on which one is invited to sit (normally cross-legged) and contemplate. These are gardens meant to be thought about, never walked in.

As in so many Zen gardens, in Tokai-an, there is a dialogue at work between gravel and rock. It can take many hundreds or even millions of years for wind and water to wear down rock into grains of sand. A few prominent rocks set amidst gravel, therefore, speak to us of time, its passage and the futility of resistance to it. What now seems so solid, individual and prominent will inevitably – through the ineluctable processes of nature – be eroded away and merged into an anonymous, undifferentiated collective.

Eihei Dōgen (1200–1253), the 13th-century monk who began Zen Buddhism in Japan, devoted his teachings to the acceptance of impermanence. Everything is impermanent, he stressed, even the moon, even Buddha, even ourselves … The thought is entirely counterintuitive. Our non-existence continues to seem the most unlikely of concepts. We assume that we are as solid as the world around us. We think of ourselves as inviolable residents rather than desperately fragile visitors. We cannot keep in mind how long the universe has been in existence and how obscure and petty will be our passage across it.

Rocks and gravel do not directly say anything to us, but they are supremely eloquent receptacles in which to entertain thoughts of our fugitiveness and the boundless dimensions of time and space. As ever with Zen Buddhism, an activity like gardening exists at both a material and a spiritual level. Raking gravel in fine lines – known as *hōkime* – aspires to save us from delusion. Zen Buddhists designed some of the finest gardens in the world, but they had no concept of themselves as gardeners. They were always, in essence, philosophers looking around for new ways of tying our thoughts back to critical truths, and using whatever was to hand – even some rock and gravel – to remind us of the path to calm and detachment.

VII.
Islam

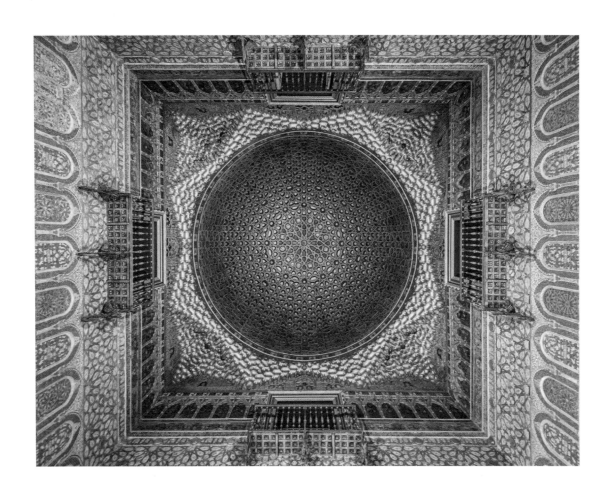

Ceiling of the Hall of the
Ambassadors, Alcázar, Seville,
Spain, 1427

1.

Islam stands out among religions by its firm insistence that artists must never resort to making pictures of Allāh. In almost every other faith, images of gods have been rife: artists have competed among themselves to depict their chief deity as an illustrious person, usually a he, often with a beard, looking like a cross between a grandfather and a favourite strict, yet wise, teacher.

For Islam, such attempts to represent Allāh will lead an artist to try – in effect – to create the creator, an ultimate act of idolatry. As the Qur'an insists: 'There is nothing whatever like Allāh'. God exceeds all comprehension; God is neither he nor she, neither human nor animal in form; God has no beginning or end, no scale or age, no dimensions or home. No mere mind can ever begin to make sense of Allāh's greatness, profundity or transcendent power – let alone set about trying to fix such infinite qualities in an image.

Insofar as Islamic artists ever tried to direct our minds to holiness, they did so with great ingenuity through what is termed the geometrical or mathematical sublime. They made abstract patterns of astonishing complexity. Thousands of interlocking circles were arranged in symmetrical associations whose underlying order we can intimate but never quite determine. Staring up at the Hall of the Ambassadors in the Alcázar in Seville (or at the Sheikh Lotfollah Mosque in Isfahan), we feel ourselves in the presence of a sovereign intelligence that is organised, disciplined, endlessly complicated and yet ultimately beyond our reason. We are awed, dizzy and newly aware of our minuteness and finitude. This – Islamic art is telling us – is one way to feel closer to God.

But there is an irony in Islam's approach to the non-representation of God. Though it understood itself to be acting out of strict piety, its philosophy has – strangely – provided an almost perfect opening for those among us who don't in any way believe. Secular people may end up far better able to relate to the God of Islam than to that of any other religion. That's because, to the extent that they ever feel a twinge of a 'religious' emotion, it tends to be in the presence of exactly the sort of abstract, vast and incomprehensible phenomena that Islam identified with Allāh. For example, when we look up at the night sky and reflect on a universe that is 13.799±0.021 billion years old, with an observable radius of 46.5 billion light-years.

It is when contemplating the extremes of high-energy particle physics or galactic astronomy that people who would never dream of praying to a well-drawn man with a beard may – for the first time – start to feel the need for a concept akin to the Islamic God in order to capture forces that eclipse every parameter of the mind.

The architects and artists of Islam may have thought of themselves as exclusively in the service of the creed of the Prophet Muhammad. Even so, their work has a special power to touch those among us for whom 'belief' is, in the end, best understood as a form of solemn respect for whatever cosmic spectacle defies humanity in terms of mystery, age, scale, intricacy and intelligence.

Medallion carpet known as 'The
Ardabil Carpet', Iran, 1539–1540

2

The so-called Ardabil Carpet – now in the Victoria and Albert Museum in London – is one of the largest and most beautiful Islamic carpets ever made. Completed in around 1540 in the Ardabil province of north-western Iran, it was commissioned by Iran's ruler Shah Tahmasp for the shrine of his ancestor, Shaykh Safi al-Din. It measures 10.5 by 5.3 metres and is exceptionally densely woven, with some 5,300 knots in every 10 square centimetres – or just under 295 million knots in total. Teams of ten weavers working in tandem took at least two years of continuous work to finish it.

The carpet's emotional power stems from the interplay of two elements that are central to Islam's overall message to us. On the one hand, the rug is delicate and warm-hearted. It is filled with garlands and trellises of flowers, those minor apparitions of nature that we all too easily tread underfoot and that chiefly catch the eye of tender spirits attuned to a vulnerable and fragile kind of goodness.

Yet, at the same time, the carpet is a work of power. It was obviously an immense undertaking, and we still sense the might of its royal patronage – especially in its indigo borders and symmetrical cartouches. In a single object, it captures a key Islamic concept, the union of love and strength, gentleness and passion. Early observers of Islam were struck by this surprising duality. A religion that knew how to fight with determination also venerated the quiet beauties of nature and thoughtful expressions of the intellect: it was interested in gardening, in the writing of poems about love and loss, in delicate decoration and refined clothing and pottery.

In this duality, Islam appears to have achieved a balance of which most of us are rarely capable. Those among us who know how to be sensitive and open to mild and subtle expressions of the spirit also tend to be regularly crushed and destroyed by the brutal juggernaut of worldly existence. And at the same time, those among us who know how to survive and fight seldom have any reserves of mind left to notice, let alone embroider, classic Persian flowers like the hyacinth or the rose.

Islam at its highest moments was able deftly to juggle strength and vulnerability. In the Mughal courts of India, warrior princes laid down their weapons and sat on the grass discussing philosophy with scholars in the shade of Chinar trees. Emperors commissioned painters to depict narcissi and composed lyrical sonnets by moonlight – before sending out trade missions and building networks of forts.

What moves us in the carpet is an ideal of how we ourselves might approach our trials – with a vigour that does not imperil our sensitivity. It models for us, in the language of knotted vegetal forms, a psychological attitude we might want to take out into our relationships or our working lives, one where strength would remain in equilibrium with susceptibility.

Islam was not ashamed to recognise that among the noblest things we might defend – and later enshrine in an enduring work of art – are a cluster of newly opened spring flowers that whisper with unaffected charm of the virtues of sweetness and humility.

The garden of Ganjali Khan
Caravanserai, Kerman, Iran

3.

It is a notable feature of many Islamic countries that their peoples tend to show exceptional hospitality to guests, especially strangers. No sooner has a visitor arrived in an Iranian home than they are likely to be offered a slice of *kuku bademjan*, some *halva* or saffron ice cream. Despite the guest's protestations, the hosts will run to the kitchen for some *lavashak* and refreshing yogurt *doogh* – and the guest almost certainly won't be able to get away without succumbing to one or two (or even a whole box for the journey) of *bamie*, the traditional deep-fried dough soaked in sugar syrup. An Egyptian dinner table will be laden with enough *kamounia* and *kofta*, *sabanekh* and *mesaqa'ah*, *ladida* and *melabbes* to feed a group ten times the size of the one actually visiting.

The abundance and the attention is not coincidental. The concept of *dyafa*, or hospitality, is vital to Islamic teaching. The Qur'an is filled with exhortations to open one's hearth to visitors and to ensure that they are made to feel in every way comfortable. We hear that the Prophet Muhammad, even in the midst of his immense responsibilities in Medina, always made time to sit down with strangers and ensure that his visitors were amply fed.

In the spirit of these teachings, Islamic countries began to build a network of unusual institutions – from Morocco to Azerbaijan, Turkey to Spain – called *caravanserai*. These were versions of hotels, where travellers could sleep and eat. Significantly, most of these *caravanserai* were built in the grand and formal styles of mosques. They had libraries, prayer rooms and paradise-like gardens. The caravanserais might have offered material sustenance, but they were – unlike modern hotels – centrally interested in the nurturing of the spirit. Those who ran them were not merely innkeepers; they wished to help to reawaken visitors' sensitivities and encourage them in the direction of thoughtfulness, piety and mercy.

If Islam spent so much effort emphasising kindness to strangers, it was because – in its theology – it believed that all of us are, once we throw off our pride and our vanity, ultimately defenceless pilgrims, who depend on the charity of others to survive. Kindness between humans is mandated by Islam because it rests on a proper acknowledgement of our shared vulnerability and need – from which only God can, in the end, deliver us. According to Islamic belief, in helping our fellow humans we are, in effect, recognising our submission to, and dependence upon, divine force.

The needs of a hungry traveller are emblematic of the incompleteness of our species. To give someone a yogurt drink and a honey cake means exercising the kind of compassion and generosity on which humanity as a whole depends. When we warmly understand a guest's needs – when we guess they might be craving some pomegranate juice, or need a cushion to support their back, or might appreciate a bit of time alone – we are extending our empathetic powers and detecting the craving, anxiety and weakness beneath the outwardly competent adult.

Islam would say we are doing God's work. We might simply say that we are being extremely nice – and that, in its own way, without anything supernatural being meant by the word, may be just as divine.

Patio de Arrayanes, The Comares
Palace, the Alhambra, Granada, Spain,
14th century

One of the more surprising and easily forgotten aspects of European history is that, for some 800 years, the Iberian peninsula was under Islamic rule. Regions that we now associate exclusively with Catholicism awoke every day to the sound of the muezzin. People spoke Arabic and dressed in *jubbas* (long coats) and *babuj* slippers in the streets of Ronda and Saragossa. There were flourishing mosques in Toledo (the Mezquita Bab-al-Mardum) and Seville (the Almohad Mosque). Córdoba, then the largest city in Europe, was a more important centre of Islamic culture than Baghdad or Cairo. And this was not a brief blip in the history of the continent: its span was as long as the period between our own age and that of Genghis Khan.

It isn't naive or idealistic to conclude that, by most measures, Islamic Europe was a hugely progressive force in the history of humankind. While most of Christian Europe had been stuck in internecine warfare and poverty since the fall of Rome, its Islamic counterpart flourished in peace and cultural freedom. Sumptuous public baths, libraries, schools and palaces were built. There were major developments in the arts and sciences. Islamic Europe developed agronomy, pharmacology and astronomy. Al-Andalus, as the region was known, was home to medical pioneers like Ibn al-Baytar (1197–1248) and Abu al-Qasim al-Zahrawi (936–1013), and astronomers like Ibn Tufayl (1110–1185) and Nur ad-Din al-Bitruji (c. 1150–1204). A sophisticated court culture gave patronage to philosophers like Averroes (1126–1198) and Maimonides (1138–1204) (the latter, a Jew, would also serve as the personal physician of Sultan Saladin). Christians and Jews were granted unparalleled degrees of freedom and status. Important Sephardic families like the de Botons, the Montefiores and the Abulafias held key offices of state, administered an efficient and fair system of taxation and ran successful trading houses.

In the countryside, agriculture was transformed through new forms of terracing and irrigation brought from the Middle East. Cotton, rice, sugar, artichokes and oranges were grown for the first time: the south of Spain became filled with lemon and fig trees. In the cities, architects created masterpieces like the Medina al-Zahra in Córdoba and the Real (Royal) Alcázar in Seville.

The aesthetic appeal of Islamic Europe was not accidental. Those marble reflecting pools in the Alhambra palace in Granada and the carvings on the minarets of Seville did not come about by chance. They were the outward expressions of an uncommonly sophisticated culture that understood how to house and reward sensitivity and intelligence.

Barbarism has never exclusively belonged to any one culture, but we can fairly propose that with the surrender of Muhammad XII and the collapse of the Emirate of Granada in 1492, civilisation took a sizeable step backwards. Within only a short time, the newly victorious Christian forces would decimate Central and South America, wipe out the reigning tolerant polyglot intellectual spirit, crush artistic expression, reduce the inventiveness of the local diet and build pompous leaden works of architecture on the foundations of ethereal palaces. In many ways, the wrong side won.

Europe has complained about Islam ever since. What it has chosen to forget is that for many generations, the continent itself nurtured a version of Islam that was every bit the equal of the high points of its own pagan and Christian eras. Many clues to the shape of a better future for both Islam and the West lie in the gardens, orchards, libraries and staterooms of the forgotten kingdoms of Al-Andalus.

VIII.
Europe

Fra Filippo Lippi, *Madonna and Child with Two Angels*, c. 1460–1465

1

Christianity had been making pictures for a very long time when, beginning in the early 14th century, a remarkable development unfolded in the Italian peninsula. In the Catacombs of Rome, early Christian artists had scratched out depictions of Jesus, Joseph and Mary on damp plaster walls; in Byzantine churches, they had assembled lambs, lions, phoenixes and fish out of mosaics. Crucifixes had been chiselled out of granite in monasteries on Iona and Skellig Michael. Then, beginning in Tuscany and spreading in time to Venice and Rome, painters hit upon an idea that would transform the history of Western art: they started to draw figures that looked not only faithful and pious, but also, as importantly, attractive. Renaissance Italy hit on the hugely original – and quietly revolutionary – notion of making the figures of the New Testament look sexy.

The move is easy to miss, but if one considers the span of Italian religious art, it is entirely implausible for anyone to seek to invite Mary on a date before 1320 – and highly unusual not to aspire to do so in the centuries thereafter. The most devoted and melancholy character in the gospels quietly evolved into a fashionable sex symbol.

The reason why has to do with ancient Greek texts. A number of manuscripts by Plato and Plotinus were uncovered in the period that laid out a distinctive theory of the mind: they proposed that we are all, first and foremost, creatures of the senses, impressed by what is beautiful, glittering and aesthetically seductive. If we are in the business of trying to convince someone of something, we must, therefore, pay great attention not just or primarily to the soundness of our arguments, but also to our outward appearance. It is all very well to deliver a lecture on the virtue of Mary, but in order to make a real impression, we should ensure, as Filippo Lippi (c. 1406–1469) did, that she can charm our eyes as well. Beauty must be brought into the service of truth and wisdom. The greatest ideas depend for their success on a capacity to awaken our senses and touch our passions.

Which explains why – during the period of art we know as the Renaissance – Christian artists produced works that were simultaneously exceptionally pious and exceptionally beautiful. The painters understood that attractiveness and sexuality were to be co-opted to the project of seducing the soul.

The modern world has – to its detriment – lost sight of this union. Those who create beauty work in one camp, while those who handle important ideas labour in another. It seldom occurs to either group to imagine how much more effective they could be if they operated together: if the most seductive image-makers joined forces with those who turn out the best ideas.

The idea of using sex 'to sell' can sound repugnant to high-minded people. Renaissance painters understood that to win someone over through sexual allure can be a highly principled activity, so long as the things being sold are dignified and important. With the Renaissance as an example, the world awaits a reconciliation between Truth and Beauty.

Giovanni and Bartolomeo Bon (also
spelled Buon), Ca' d'Oro, Grand
Canal, Venice, Italy, completed 1436

2.

Christianity was, from its inception, highly convinced that making money was a regrettable and impious activity, likely to take us away from God, encourage pride and harden our hearts. Christians made money – sometimes a lot of it – but almost always with a guilty conscience and a degree of furtiveness. The lessons of Jesus with the money-changers sank deep.

Then, starting in the Italian peninsula in the 13th century, attitudes began to shift. Partly, the evolution was dependent on practical changes: merchants assumed ever more power relative to monarchs, trade routes opened up with the East, new and faster ships were developed, double-entry book-keeping was invented, early forms of joint stock companies were pioneered and syndicates of wealthy families joined together to finance larger enterprises. These were material developments that histories of finance have been adept at tracing. But they were ultimately a consequence of new ideas about money: how to evaluate its worth and judge its role in human affairs.

It came to be recognised that certain projects of indubitable value could not be possible without money. Certainly, there was something a little demeaning and vain about trade: about spending the majority of one's conscious hours accumulating ducats from the sale of salted cod or anchovies, or in thinking almost exclusively about how to arrange a workshop making lace for evening dresses. Nevertheless, without such exertions, a lot that was evidently necessary would have to be sacrificed: there could be no churches for the faithful, no hospitals for the poor and no elegant squares for the citizenry. Venice's Ospedale degli Incurabili had been indirectly funded by trade in sugar, silk and alum.

The great cities of Renaissance Italy nuanced their Christian doctrines accordingly. There was no longer any need for continuous guilt. What mattered was not how much money individuals made, but how judiciously, kindly and imaginatively they were able to spend it – how many painters they were able to fund, how many hospitals they could endow and how many scholars they could support.

The new equilibrium was especially felt in Venice. This was a city exceptionally interested in becoming rich, but – as its plethora of churches, medical institutes and gracious public spaces attest – it was also, for a time, exceptionally interested in directing money to the finest ends.

The Contarini family were to Venice what the Medicis were to Florence: an ancient family that was invested in spending its money not just for private satisfaction, but for the greater glory of their city. Their family home, the Ca' d'Oro, constructed on the Grand Canal in the 1420s and 1430s and arguably the most beautiful Venetian house ever built, remains an emblem of how wealth may be put to work in the name of a refinement and sensitivity that benefits a whole city rather than merely those who control its resources.

We have in our own times shed all inhibitions about making money; more tragically, we appear to have lost any sense of the imperative to spend it intelligently. We look constantly at who has made large sums; we almost never enquire what they have found to do with it. It's an attitude that would have shocked and saddened Cosimo de' Medici or Ermolao Barbaro. Italy in its golden age reminds us that societies reach true greatness when they devote as much thought to expenditure as to accumulation. There remain far too few Venices – and far too many Las Vegases.

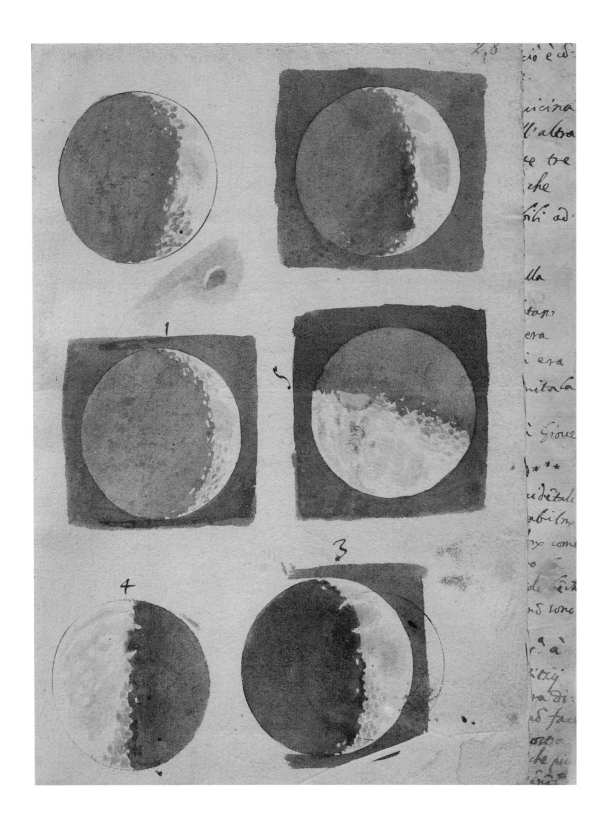

Galileo Galilei, *Six depictions
of the moon*, 1609

3.

Though it has been in the sky for a while, for most of human history no one was especially interested in looking very much – or at least very closely – at the moon. The ancient Sumerians took a quick look and decided that the moon was a god of wisdom called Nanna; for the ancient Egyptians, it was a god called Khonsu, meaning 'traveller' and for the ancient Greeks, it was self-evidently a goddess called Selene, daughter of the Titans Hyperion and Theia, and sister of the goddess of dawn, Eos, and of the sun god Helios.

Despite these conflicting certainties, the one thing that all traditional cultures were united on was the need not to study the subject any further. It is, therefore, hard to overestimate the significance of what happened on the night of 30 November 1609, when a hitherto obscure professor of mathematics at the university of Padua pointed his telescope up at the moon – and had the first open-minded, scientifically ego-less look at our Earth's natural satellite. Galileo Galilei had heard about the (then) astonishing new instrument called a telescope that had been produced in the Netherlands the year before, and had found a way to grind lenses and produce a version with a 20× linear magnification. Through this optical marvel, he quickly realised that the old stories about the moon were nonsense. This was not the flawless, marble-like orb evoked in the Old Testament's Song of Solomon, nor the pearl evoked by Dante, nor the spiritual counterpart to the Virgin Mary dear to Catholicism.

What Galileo's telescope told him, indisputably, was that the surface of the moon was pitted and mottled. He concluded that the uneven waning of the moon must be caused by light occlusion from some very high mountains and extremely wide craters, which he assiduously drew with an accuracy that impresses to this day. (He also estimated for the first time that the moon's radius was 1,600 kilometres – not far off the 1,740 kilometres we know of now.)

It must have been tempting for Galileo to doubt himself. Everyone – from the Pope to his fellow academics to members of his own family – was sure that he was wrong, and told him so with force. All the same, Galileo went ahead and published a small book, *Sidereus Nuncius* (Starry Messenger) in which he insisted on his ideas – and also (to further consternation) threw in the suggestion that Jupiter had four moons rather than the presumed three.

The story continues to speak to us because – though we may have little interest in astronomy – it mirrors a conflict that we all face between what the world insists is normal and true, and the sometimes diverging evidence of our own senses and suppositions. Galileo might have flouted public opinion in relation to heavenly bodies; we are more likely to run into opposition around marriage, work or politics. The issues will be different, but the strength of character the challenges demand will be identical.

Much about social life conspires to keep us cowed and timid. Without becoming a crank or obsessive, by trusting reason and deduction, one of the iconic figures of early modern Europe prompts us to imagine how much madness and error might lie within what is innocently called common sense.

Jean-Baptiste-Siméon Chardin,
The Governess, c. 1739

4

Governesses were employed in most aristocratic houses in early modern France. They administered the domestic finances, managed the cook and – most importantly – looked after the children. They entered service in their late teens, seldom married and largely lived and died in obscurity. History was made by, and was about, other people: kings and queens, martyrs and saints, warriors and poets.

But, from the 17th century onwards, in Holland, England and France, a new sort of art emerged that focused on the lives of so-called ordinary people: men and women engaged in arranging the laundry cupboard or sweeping the yard, preparing dinner or repairing a cart. A message emerged in art long before it would be manifest in politics: that modest destinies contained as much value and dignity as prominent ones.

The painter Jean-Baptiste-Siméon Chardin (1699–1779) was known as a master of *la vie silencieuse* (the silent life). His central figures are almost all of negligible means. He could not transform their incomes, but he dramatically altered their status, battling the prejudices of those who would condemn the underprivileged for lacking a formal education or a title.

For most of his life, the aristocrat on the left of Chardin's painting would be the one to attract admiration and interest. At this particular moment in his childhood, however, guided by a painter of genius, we focus our attention on his governess. We sense her tenderness and gentle manner. We know she is full of intelligence, however little she may have read. She would not be one to lose her temper easily or come to rash judgements, but we also know that the boy has not behaved as he should – and he knows it too, as his blushing cheeks attest. The games on the bottom left indicate that school work has been neglected. Latin verbs or prayers may have been ignored or thank you letters left unwritten: this is surely no way for my sweet one to behave?

In later years, the aristocrat may command armies and make grown men tremble. Now, he has to bow his head in shame and acknowledge his errors – and try a little harder to be good. The governess will be easy to ignore when he is older. He might pay her the odd visit and, on the day a footman arrives with news of her death in a small cottage in the provinces, regret how long it was since he last saw her. Yet we know how much he should be in her debt – and the extent to which any future sanity and kindness he can lay claim to will be down to her.

The scene we see in the painting was taking place fifty years before the French Revolution and its aspirations for fraternity and equality – but, in art, with a great deal more success and kindness, a place of redemptive humanity and sympathy had already been reached.

Maurice Quentin de La Tour, *Portrait
of la marquise de Pompadour* ('Madame
Pompadour'), 1752–1755

5.

It is self-evident how much more civilised the world has – in many areas – grown with time. And yet at moments, we catch an attitude or practice in the lives of our forebears that may fairly leave us thoughtful and questioning whether we truly are as worldly, open-minded or advanced as we are fond of believing.

Madame de Pompadour was the official mistress of Louis XV of France between 1745 and 1751. He had married his wife, Marie Leszczyńska, Queen of France, at the age of fifteen (she was twenty-two) but after twenty years of conjugal life, matters had cooled. He respected her highly still, but his longings ran in other directions. The modern age tends to deem such situations a tragedy and will swiftly suggest initiating costly and ruinous divorce proceedings that may forever poison relations and embitter spouses and children. Louis, Marie and their circle were a great deal more sophisticated and imaginative than that.

They understood Louis and his wife's needs – but also how much affection still held them together. Louis, therefore, began a relationship with Madame de Pompadour, which everyone at court knew about and which shocked no one. The Queen and her circle accepted her warmly – and the two women often met to discuss matters of state, as well as art and music, subjects about which they were both highly knowledgeable. The Queen also took a lover. There was respect and kindness all around. No one was humiliated or hurt. Louis and Madame de Pompadour were free to enjoy their mutual desires (and an intellectual connection too) while the King and Queen's bond deepened into a tender friendship.

Our cult of romantic love – which began in the West towards the end of the 18th century – makes it almost impossible for us to accept such a situation. We have indelibly wedded together love and sex. We cannot imagine desiring one person while loving another. After twenty contented years together, we favour declaring a marriage over the moment there might be lassitude in the bedroom.

The earlier Classical age made no such dogmatic errors. It understood that love has its phases, that the time of passionate *eros* can be succeeded by temperate and loyal *philia* without anyone being harmed or insulted. Our rigidity has forced innumerable couples who would, under a different ideology, have thought themselves worthy and fortunate into the divorce courts.

We might imagine that Louis XV was able to behave as he did because he was the king. In fact, he was only following what many in his class – women as well as men – assumed to be a sensitive and respectful response to the complexities of relationships. We pride ourselves on being a good deal more 'romantic' than our ancestors; in reality, we may simply be operating with a far narrower, more one-dimensional and ultimately more cruel idea of what it means to love.

Thomas Rowlandson, *The Successful
Fortune Hunter, or Captain Shelalee
Leading Miss Marrowfat to the Temple
of Hymen*, 1802

6

Thomas Rowlandson (1756–1827) was the foremost cartoonist of Britain's Georgian era – and a genius of wit and cruelty. In over 10,000 drawings, he laid into every conceivable absurdity of his time. His targets included the royal family, lecherous priests, French people, pompous military generals, the nouveau riche, spoilt children, farting grandfathers, more French people, drunken judges, Napoleon, syphilis-addled whores and thieving art dealers.

Perhaps his favourite objects of satire were couples who had married for the 'wrong' reasons. That meant, people who wed for reasons other than love: for money, for company, for status, for children, out of fear of loneliness or to please their parents. It is worth recognising the novelty of the idea of 'love matches'. The world has come to side so overwhelmingly with Rowlandson's implicit assessment of them that we may forget their originality, their ambition – and their complications.

For most of history, people had, without any shame or compunction, married one another for entirely unromantic reasons: because someone had a castle or access to a plough, because their parents knew your parents, because God or the state had demanded it … The last thing that anyone worried about was whether or not one happened to be filled with longing and desire for one's partner at the altar. It was assumed that dizzying feelings were not to be trusted anyway, and that in time, with a fair wind, one would grow fond enough of the candidate whom rational and cautionary reasons had pushed one towards. Love was seen as a typical – although not universal nor necessary – consequence of marriage, never its precondition.

Then, thanks to the efforts of proselytising poets and artists, a new thesis on love came to the fore. The only basis on which to make a respectable marriage was, it now appeared, a firm conviction of the overwhelming inner and outer beauty of the beloved. Hence Rowlandson's merciless laughter at his unfortunate couple: we are being prompted to chuckle at how corrupt he is for marrying someone because she might have a house and enough money to get by, and how desperate she is for marrying someone because he is tall and kind and she doesn't want to die alone. What rascals!

We tend to think of the pre-19th-century view of marriage as abominably restrictive, but along the way, we miss the fact that the romantic ideal of love that succeeded it was in its way just as snobbish and tricky. It was – and remains – ruthless towards anyone who can't match its strict dictates: anyone who might be tempted to stay in a marriage because they are afraid of being on their own or worry that the children might get hurt, or who gets together with someone not because the partner exhausts their imagination, but because they are friendly enough and it's no fun to spend every weekend alone.

The cult of emotional ecstasy was meant to liberate us; but it has become a trap of its own. It has left many people, perhaps a silent majority, wondering what is wrong with them for not being able to experience blinding passion along the prescribed lines.

Fortunately, a study of history shows us that those who are guilty of what romantics call 'compromising' in love are not necessarily insane or weak; they have, perhaps, just understood themselves, their options and reality far better than our dogmatic age is able to admit.

Quirijn van Brekelenkam, *Sentimental Conversation*, early 1660s

7

A handsome young officer has come to pay a visit – as he suggested he would. Perhaps they met at a ball and he slipped her a note, or their eyes locked at the theatre, or she knows his cousin in The Hague. Now he's been here just under half an hour and his manner has relaxed. He played her a little ditty on the violin, he suggested a jug of wine be brought in, he explained to her about a military manoeuvre he took part in during a campaign against the Spanish near Antwerp when he and two fellow-officers went behind enemy lines and they managed to blow up an ammunition dump. He's opened his legs and told her that she has a very pretty mouth.

For her, it's all hugely new and unexpected – and undeniably thrilling as well. She was brought up at a strict Protestant boarding school in Eindhoven, and the teachers told her to stay well clear of this sort of character. Her father – who died last year – would probably not have approved either. But now it's her and her mother and two younger sisters and she can't deny that he has a very handsome jaw and attractive grey trousers. Furthermore, she read a lot of poetry under the covers – mostly German and French writers – and her heart has been attuned to these sort of feelings. She suspects she has begun to blush uncontrollably.

The artist, Quirijn van Brekelenkam (d. 1669), is only too aware of what is at stake. This is no game. It may be the start of a nightmare. Behind the woman is a troubling painting of rocks, fast-flowing streams, clouds and what might be a volcanic eruption. The moral is clear: there could be a lot of trouble ahead. She might relent too easily; he could take advantage of her and her reputation would be gone in twenty minutes. His confidence might spill over into arrogance and her gentleness into fateful naivety. Women don't understand too much about men; and vice versa. Every year, prospective couples are unleashed into the world without any sense of what they are letting themselves in for.

What can strike contemporary observers of the painting is how little – in spite of so many developments – has changed. Headstrong young seducers still approach somewhat overly trusting victims and make promises they won't keep. The very same scene unfolds in a hundred nightclubs and university dorm rooms, as satellites orbit overhead and nuclear-powered submarines keep the peace. Modernity has not reached love.

We still lack the education in the emotions that would stop us making unfortunate choices in relationships and could help us to understand ourselves and our needs before it is too late. We choose partners on the basis of feelings that are opaque to us. We may be compelled towards someone by a secret wish to re-create patterns of suffering and doubt that we knew as children; our lack of self-esteem may push us towards candidates who we unconsciously sense will not like us any more than we like ourselves.

We will know that we have collectively made true progress with our emotions when this picture can – at last – look as old-fashioned as it should.

François Xavier Vispré,
*Portrait of a Man Reclining on
a Sofa, Reading*, 1750

8

It looks like such an ordinary scene that we're apt to miss its strangeness, its newness – and its message to our own times. A man is reading on the sofa. He's wearing some comfortable slippers and a day jacket. He's got a further five books and two pamphlets to go if he were to finish or get bored.

The habit of lounging on sofas was a novelty in itself. Priests had sermonised against it; mothers had warned their daughters not to indulge lest their virtue be tainted. The bigger novelty, though, is that our man is reading. People had, of course, been reading for a very long time. The Middle Ages was filled with devout monks and scribes poring over holy texts; prayer books had been part of daily life for many centuries. What was unique to the 18th century was the idea of reading secular texts for pleasure, of lying back at home for many hours and silently communing with an author who didn't want to speak about God or Hell but about adventures on other continents, the puzzles of science and the thrilling deeds of nations.

The price of books had kept falling ever since the 16th century; new circulating libraries had emerged in most European countries by the 1720s. It wasn't technical change alone, however, that had created what Germans at the time referred to as a *Lesewut* or 'reading craze'. What really made the difference was how books started to be written. The 18th-century reading revolution was powered by a new ideal of readability. Joseph Addison (1672–1719), founder of England's *Spectator* magazine, argued in a series of highly influential articles that the task of a writer was, above all, to sound 'agreeable'. Enough of obscure academics, cryptic scientists, esoteric historians or sombre clergymen. Modern writers should be clear, direct, personable, humane, witty – and never confusing or long-winded.

Addison mounted a passionate protest against the long-standing belief that the hallmark of a clever person is that nobody can understand what they are saying ... or that intelligent books should never be easy to read.

His clarion call helped to set a new intellectual tone for his age: 'popular' was no longer to be a damning word. It was merely evidence that a writer had understood their craft.

In England, new ranks of fiction-loving sofa-readers could now indulge in such fluent works as Daniel Defoe's *Robinson Crusoe* (1719), Jonathan Swift's *Gulliver's Travels* (1726) and Samuel Richardson's *Pamela* (1740). In France, they enjoyed the Abbé Prévost's *Manon Lescaut* (1731), Voltaire's *Candide* (1759) and Rousseau's *La Nouvelle Héloïse* (1761); in Germany, they wept in their millions over *The Sorrows of Young Werther* (1774). It wasn't only fiction that grew so readable. Between 1754 and 1761 David Hume published *The History of England*, a six-volume work spanning 'From the Invasion of Julius Caesar to the Revolution in 1688', which was as excitingly paced as a novel while remaining scrupulously accurate and serious; in France, Voltaire's *History of Charles XII* (1731) and *The Age of Louis XIV* (1751) pulled off a similar balancing act.

Book sales have continued to rise ever since, but we may still look back at the 18th century with nostalgia because it was the first – and arguably the last – era to have believed so wholeheartedly in the idea of a literary union between seriousness and popularity. Thereafter, the two qualities were separated once again: writers could be clever, wise – and unread. Or they could be racy, dumb – and popular. They could not easily be authors of intelligent bestsellers. The great 18th-century writers – Hume, Defoe, Voltaire, Gibbon, Rousseau among them – stand out to this day through their admixture of complexity and charm. One can lean back on the sofa with them, without ever quite realising the extent to which one is being educated and enhanced.

It is always an achievement to write a clever book; the 18th century knew (and continues to remind us) that it is an even greater and rarer feat to ensure it is a painless and entertaining one as well.

IX.
The Americas

XIII.

Their manner of fishynge in Virginia.

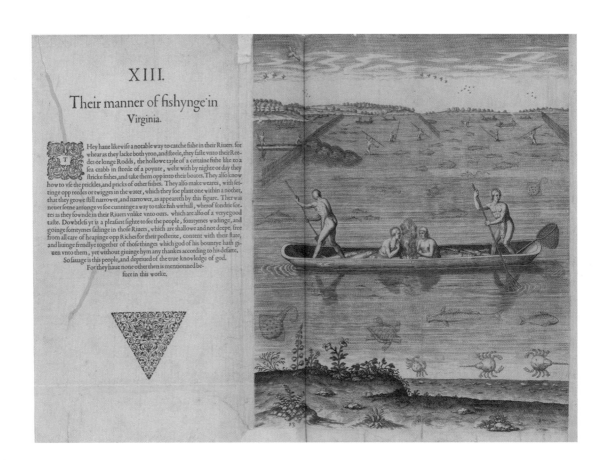

T Hey haue likewise a notable way to catche fishe in their Riuers. for wheras they lacke both yron, and steele, they faste vnto their Reedes or longe Rodds, the hollowe tayle of a certaine fishe like to a sea crabb in steede of a poynte, wehr with by nighte or day they stricke fishes, and take them opp into their boates. They also know how to vse the prickles, and pricks of other fishes. They also make weares, with settinge opp reedes or twigges in the water, which they soe plant one within a nother, that they growe still narrower, and narrower, as appeareth by this figure. Ther was neuer seene amonge vs soe cunninge a way to take fish withall, wherof sondrie sortes as they fownde in their Riuers vnlike vnto ours. which are also of a verye good taste. Dowbtless yt is a pleasant sighte to see the people, somtymes wadinge, and goinge somtymes sailinge in those Riuers, which are shallowe and not deepe, free from all care of heapinge opp Riches for their posterite, content with their state, and liuinge frendlye together of those thinges which god of his bountye hath giuen vnto them, yet without giuinge hym any thankes according to his desarte. So sauage is this people, and depriued of the true knowledge of god. For they haue none other then is mentionned before in this worke.

'Their manner of fishynge in Virginia.' Engraving by Theodore de Bry based on watercolour by John White, in *A Briefe and True Report of the New Found Land of Virginia*, written by Thomas Harriot, 1590

1.

On 26 June 1585, a flotilla of ships under the command of the English explorer Sir Ralph Lane landed on Roanoke Island on the Outer Banks of North Carolina. They had sailed to America – with the blessing of the English monarch, Elizabeth I – with the intention of starting a new colony, from which it was hoped riches and prestige would flow. On board were a talented artist named John White (fl. 1585–1593) and an equally skilled and curious writer, Thomas Harriot (1560–1621). While the other colonists began to build themselves houses (and a church), the two men went out to map the local territory and, most momentously, to befriend the locals.

They were Algonquin Indians – and though they looked very different from anyone whom White or Harriot had ever met, they led a way of life that quickly struck the Englishmen as particularly intelligent and sane. They dwelt in small, neat villages near the coast; the men spent a few hours fishing every day, and the women took care of clothing, the houses and the children. Their food was plentiful and nutritious. They made interesting music; their rugs were beautiful. In the evening, they would sit around the fire singing songs, dancing and smoking long thin pipes. They were affectionate and peaceable, their features were open and pleasant, they had a ready laugh – and loved to play practical jokes on their new acquaintances.

White and Harriot spent months researching their lives and, on their return to England, produced an illustrated book that forever altered the European imagination. It was the first complete description of a figure who would go on to play an immense and complex role in our understanding of our needs and of the meaning of life: someone who came to be known as the 'noble savage'.

Europeans knew that they had the upper hand technologically: they had the ships, the swords and the horses. And yet the Native Americans they encountered appeared to be significantly happier, freer and healthier than they were. Was there something that, despite all of Europe's advantages, they were missing? In the rush to become 'civilised', had the West misunderstood itself?

In the coming centuries, philosophers were to pore over the examples of these tribes in search of answers to what modern civilisation, for all its wealth, might have failed to grasp about its true needs. Among other ideas, there were proposals that perhaps the so-called Indians were more content because they didn't live in cities, because they spent more time with their families, because they breast-fed their children, because their food was simpler, because their religions didn't speak so much about Hell, because their jobs felt meaningful to them, because they didn't read newspapers or compare themselves to others and because there wasn't so much for them to buy and want and therefore to feel inadequate without.

In the example of the Native Americans, the more enlightened Europeans of those times came to understand their societies' own illnesses; the tribes were a mirror in which to study the avarice and neuroses of modernity. We don't need to idealise the peoples of 16th-century Virginia to accept that, almost inadvertently, they had stumbled upon, or remained loyal to, ingredients of happiness that the modern world had thrown away without realising. Their examples continue to provoke us. What would it mean to reform our own societies with their lessons in mind? What might the Algonquin people have to teach us about – for example – communal life, childcare, work, status or self-esteem? What if we learnt to be not their murderers or belittlers, but rather – as a handful of Europeans strove to be hundreds of years ago – their humble observers and careful, imaginative students?

Spiridione Roma, *The East Offering
its Riches to Britannia*, commissioned
by the East India Company, East India
House, London, 1778

2

This allegorical painting finds the West at a zenith of confidence. Britannia, a delicate young lady seated on the rock, is being offered goods by her many conquered lands. Calcutta is giving her a basket of pearls and other precious jewels, Bengal is presenting her with an elephant and a camel, China is donating a Ming vase. In the background, some shadowy figures are piling up bundles of raw cotton for her. Within a few decades of this painting being completed, Europe had conquered all of the Americas, the whole of Australia and substantial parts of Africa and Asia.

What historians have been wondering about, and arguing over, ever since is why. Why was it Britannia (or France or Spain) sitting smugly on a rock while the world gave her riches, and not the other way around? Why wasn't it an Iroquois Indian or a Powhatan princess receiving roast beef and bales of wool from a ragged and subjugated England? Why weren't Portugal or Spain on their knees offering to do whatever the Incas or the Caribs wanted?

The answer the victors gave at the time was simple: God had willed it. God had wanted Portugal to seize Brazil and England to make itself at home in Virginia. These victors also proposed that it was because they were inherently more intelligent than those they dominated. We might instinctively bristle, but we should more wisely start to unpick one of the largest questions of the past: why were some countries historically so much more militarily successful than others?

The real answers tend to be unheroic and accidental-sounding, but all the more important for that. None of the subjugated nations had the right sort of animals; they lacked draft creatures to pull ploughs and till soil efficiently, and therefore could not release human beings to advance their technical and commercial skills. And they had nothing like horses on which to ride into battle – at best, one had to make do with a llama or a guanaco. The conquered lands tended to lie on the tropical belt where, every year, a substantial share of the most active population would be taken away by disease. Furthermore, these lands lay beyond the main east–west trade routes that facilitated the exchange not only of goods, but also of ideas and innovations. Writing, accountancy, mathematics, science, agriculture – all witnessed breakthroughs in particular places and were, with time, diffused across the entire Eurasian landmass, so that every region could benefit from the intellectual high points of its neighbours. A person in the Netherlands or Spain was – without realising it – heavily indebted to the most exceptional minds of Baghdad or Beijing. No such advantages were open to the inhabitants of Australia or South America, whom oceans and mountain ranges kept cut off from foreign brilliance. In a world where perhaps only 1 in 20 million people ever arrives at a useful idea, they were denied the lifeline of interconnection.

Lastly, European nations were exceptionally querulous. They had been trying to exterminate one another continuously for two millennia or so. Population pressures upped the belligerent tempo. The Natives of the Americas had their squabbles, but they could not possibly compete with Europe's sustained history of military aggression – and their weapons showed it. They were too ready to settle things amicably. They had too much land to fight to the death for every square centimetre of it – or to work incessantly at developing a perfectly lethal sabre.

Europeans who spent time with the conquered peoples of the Americas quickly realised that they were dealing with intellectually highly able and quick-witted minds: it is far from easy to herd bison across the plains or to build a network of roads through the Andes. The conquered peoples were the victims of quasi-accidental military weaknesses that said nothing whatsoever about their reasoning capacities or their souls. They were done in by a force for which the modern world – without admitting as much – lacks the slightest patience, interest or sympathy: very bad luck.

Engraving by Theodor de Bry, from
*A Short Account of the Destruction of
the Indies*, written by Bartolomé de
las Casas, 1598

3

What continues to be shocking about the Spanish conquest of the Americas is its speed and the scale of its destructiveness. In the hundred years that followed the arrival of Columbus on the shores of the Caribbean, it is estimated that 90 percent of the Indigenous population – 56 million people – died. That represented 10 percent of the entire population of the world at the time. (It was the most catastrophic human mortality event in history, the next being World War II, which killed 3 percent.) Most of the deaths were caused by measles, smallpox, influenza and bubonic plague, which native immune systems – cut off from Europe for the previous 13,000 years – could not cope with. However, millions were also roasted alive, cut in half, worked to death in silver and gold mines or forced to commit suicide. A small taste of the barbarism can be found in a grim masterpiece of Spanish literature, Bartolomé de las Casas' *A Short Account of the Destruction of the Indies*, (written in 1542), in which the author – a priest who witnessed the butchery at first hand – declared his countrymen unfit for God's mercy. It is one of the oddities of history that, despite comparable butchery, Spain has received not a sliver of the disapproval that has come Germany's way.

Many empires and nations have collapsed, but none quite so suddenly as those of the Aztecs and the Incas. 500 men under Hernán Cortés landed in Mexico in February 1519 and, by August 1521, had seized the whole country, captured the last Aztec emperor Cuauhtémoc and laid waste to the capital Tenochtitlán, one of the largest cities in the world, reputed to have been more beautiful than Venice. In 1528, Francisco Pizarro landed with 180 men on the northern shores of the Inca empire, which stretched from Quito in the north to Santiago in the south (the largest empire that had ever existed anywhere on Earth), and by 1533, the force had captured the emperor Atahualpa, dissolved his country and sentenced the terrified man to be burnt at the stake – though after he had allowed himself to be baptised, the kindly Spanish let him off by strangling him instead.

Bartolomé de las Casas (1484–1566) did not hesitate to call the Native Americans the equals of the Romans and the Greeks – and hugely superior to the Europeans of his own day. The surviving evidence of their architecture, literature, politics and religion bears this out. We can only lament how much richer and more interesting the world would now be if these American cultures had been given a few more years (rather than mere hours) to ready themselves for the European onslaught; if the Aztecs and the Incas had been granted some of the good fortune of, for example, the Japanese, who – due to accidents of geography – had three decades to fully open their doors to the West and so saved themselves for posterity.

Because the Japanese had time to learn about Western science and technology, we can now enjoy tea ceremonies and Zen monasteries while benefiting from bullet trains and flat screen televisions. In an alternative history, the Aztecs would similarly have had a moment of protection in which to adjust, so that Tenochtitlán could today charm visitors with its gardens and floating palaces, while modern jetliners circled Cuauhtémoc International Airport and keyhole surgery would unfold at the immaculate Ixtlilton Clinic – named after the Aztec god of medicine.

Instead, the impatient aggression of the European colonisers paved the way for an unhappy, restless monoculture that continues to search for equilibrium to this day. When Las Casas begged the Spanish king to stop his army's destruction of the New World, he used the argument that Native Americans were like young adults, who needed a little longer to be able to ready themselves to live independently alongside the nations of Europe. Spain was not to kill them like vengeful parents in the interim. We can regret aspects of the analogy – but it captures accurately and generously enough what the pre-Colombian nations of the Americas would have needed to survive: a few more years.

Jean-Michel Moreau, 'C'est a ce prix
que vous mangez du sucre en Europe'
(It is at this price that you eat
sugar in Europe), from illustrated
edition of Voltaire's *Candide*, 1787

4

One of the unwittingly absurd aspects of the conquest and destruction of the New World is what it was all, in the end, done in the name of: vanilla sponge cake with icing sugar. Plum pudding with custard. Milky tea with shortbread biscuits. Sticky toffee pudding.

All enslavement and mass murder is – of course – catastrophic, but certain examples have at least been perpetrated with a degree of (twisted) logic or a (degenerate) vision of higher ideals. Some deluded murderers have truly believed that they were doing it for God, justice or the salvation of humankind. Their actions may have been reprehensible, yet somewhere in the background lay something other than mere cynicism.

None of that is true for the Americas. It's possible to be so distracted by those iron manacles, the packed ships lifting anchor off the coast of the Gulf of Guinea, the plantation overseers in Barbados and Haiti and the oleaginous financiers in London and Bristol, that one can forget to be offended by the sheer daftness and vanity of why it all happened in the first place. It is no sign of disrespect to approach the horror with a neglected but valuable instrument: satire.

The European who best understood this was the writer and philosopher Voltaire (1694–1778). In a famous passage in *Candide* (first published 1759), the eponymous hero and his companion Cacambo come across a maimed slave on a sugar plantation. He's had his hand cut off as a punishment for getting a finger stuck in a millstone – and his leg cut off for trying to run away. Still though, the slave shows great respect for his European master – and his religion. What is all this suffering for, Candide asks? The slave sounds almost apologetic: So that you can have sugar in Europe.

The problem with cakes and their like is that they tend not to speak very much. They sit innocently on a tea table in Bath or Edinburgh and don't mention a mutilated slave under a palm tree 6,500 kilometres away. It is the task of art and politics to make the connection – and cut our appetite. This was the approach of one of the earliest and most successful consumer boycotts, William Fox's Anti-Saccharite movement in England in the 1790s. In a pamphlet called 'An Address to the People of Great Britain on the Propriety of Refraining from the Use of West India Sugar and Rum' (1791), Fox argued that ordinary consumers could not evade responsibility for millions of enslaved people on the other side of the world: a single family eating their way through 5 pounds (2.27 kilograms) of sugar a week could either save or doom the life of one slave. The pamphlet sold 130,000 copies; 400,000 people in Britain stopped eating sugar as a result. Britain abolished the slave trade in 1807.

The Anti-Saccharites understood that capitalism can best be improved not so much by attacking producers as by working on the minds of consumers. It is patterns of demand that ultimately determine what is made and how workers are treated. Their battle was to convince us of the unlikely idea that 'small things' (a cake here, a biscuit there) might truly be connected up to momentous geo-political events; that what happened in a tea room in York might have the power to affect events in Senegal and Brazil. It was also part of their plan to show us that sugar was not – in the end – any sort of indispensable ingredient of happiness. It only seemed that way to those who lacked creativity. Honey was, they pointed out, just as tasty, and several recipe books were written to prove it. Not only might sugar-eaters be destroying the world, the campaigners proposed, but also they might be doing so in the name of a flawed and inaccurate idea of happiness.

Sugar is no longer quite as problematic as it once was; but plenty of other things are. As Voltaire would have wanted us to keep asking: at what price has our happiness been bought? And, more pointedly, have we even been rendered properly happy in the first place?

Joshua Reynolds, *Portrait of
Syacust Ukah (Ostenaco)*, 1762

5

The English were the most successful colonists of the Americas, but they were also by far the most squeamish. Throughout their process of occupation, they took immense care to manage their reputations and suggest that what might have been deemed robbery was in truth a process of self-sacrifice, homage, patronage and kindness. Their manipulation allows us to study, with particular clarity, the workings of those twin delusions: sentimentality and rationalisation.

Ostenaco (1710–1780) was a Cherokee chief from Great Tellico, in Tennessee. He developed a reputation for valour among the English, on whose side he fought during the French and Indian War (1754–63), and after he expressed a desire to travel to England to meet its own great chief, he was offered, by way of thanks, a passage to London on a trading ship. His visit proved to be a sensation: all the leading aristocrats requested meetings, there were queues three hours long to get a glimpse of him, he stocked up on presents at the best shops in Piccadilly, and he narrowly avoided a diplomatic incident when, at Buckingham House, he tried to get George III to smoke his pipe of peace. Along the way, Ostenaco was painted by the leading portraitist of the day, Sir Joshua Reynolds (1723–1792), who described him as the noblest man he had ever met. Smart London agreed that Ostenaco was an epitome of honesty, straightforwardness and intelligence – and there was considerable sadness the day he had to say his farewells and sail back to America.

None of this ostensible admiration for Native Americans stopped the colonists from plundering Cherokee property, pushing them out of their demarcated lands and eventually annihilating their culture and way of life. However, all along, the English settlers remained acutely sensitive to all accusations of avarice and aggression.

To justify their position, the more intellectual among them made use of some wily political arguments by the leading philosopher of early modern England, John Locke (1632–1704). Locke's patrons had been involved in the early years of the colonisation of America and Locke, as their loyal servant, had been keen to help them to sleep better. In his *Two Treatises of Government* (1689), he had, therefore, come up with a remarkable theory of land ownership. Traditionally, the assumption had been that ownership was always conferred through occupation – which was now an awkward idea, given how long the Native Americans had been in place. Locke newly proposed that true ownership was, in fact, bequeathed only through something he called 'labour' – by which he meant European farming. Only those who enclosed, tilled and cultivated a piece of land could be thought of as its rightful owners. The Native Americans, by virtue of their reliance on hunting and the collection of wild nuts and fruits, could have no right to any land whatsoever – and so were to be legitimately dispossessed by anyone who came from England with a plough and an intention to plant a field or ten of wheat or barley.

It was an argument of near (malevolent) genius – and for a long time, it helped the English (and their post-revolutionary successors) to live easily with themselves as they set about dispossessing an entire people and continent. What was especially important to the English was that they should never in any way be compared with the Spanish or Portuguese conquerors down in South America: those were the barbarians. The English were the civilisers.

It's a reminder of the many ways in which cleverness can play a role in subtly masking, and hence ultimately aggravating, abuses and transgressions. The cause of honesty is sometimes best served by a degree of simple-mindedness. The English had too much of a conscience to plunder openly, yet not too much to want to stop doing so altogether. Their story offers a morality tale on the dangers of the use of intelligence as a means of getting away with what one might as well plainly term murder.

Unknown photographer, Chief Charlo,
Head of the Flathead or Bitterroot
Salish Tribe, Flathead Reservation,
Montana, c. 1907

6

One of the curious and melancholy accidents of history is that Native American society survived, in its traditional forms, just long enough to coincide with the invention and development of photography. The Khmer, the Sumerians, the Mayans must be resurrected in our imaginations from fragments. Native Americans, leading traditional lives outside of reservations, are there for us in the plentiful photographic archives of the 19th century.

The world's first photograph, *View from the Window at Le Gras*, was taken in 1826 by French scientist Joseph Nicéphore Niépce; four years later, the US government passed the Removal Act that forced Native Americans to give up their ancestral lands in the eastern United States and move west of the Mississippi.

So we don't need to imagine very much at all. We can see the faces of the Cherokee, Chickasaw, Choctaw, Muscogee and Seminole tribes through a medium perfectly suited both to capturing time and evoking its loss. We can see into the sorrowful, profound, defiant eyes of the Sioux chief Red Cloud, the Hunkpapa Lakota commander Sitting Bull or the Nez Perce leader Chief Joseph. Few images of those final generations, though, have quite the power of that of the Flathead Indian Chief Charlo, pictured on his horse at the Flathead Reservation in Montana in the summer of 1907.

The Flathead Indians had lived in southwestern Montana's fertile Bitterroot Valley for four centuries when the US government decided, in 1891, to pay them a modest sum to relocate to a small plot it termed the Flathead Indian Reservation in western Montana. Chief Charlo was furious – 'You had better hunt some people who want money more than we do' – but this wasn't a choice. The government at least vowed that white settlers would leave them in peace. But, as always, the promise was written in sand. In 1904, Congress passed the Flathead Allotment plan that gave whites the right to settle and farm across what had only shortly before been deemed exclusively Flathead territory.

We aren't projecting any feelings into Chief Charlo's face. Beneath his Victorian top hat and coat (he wore them for white visitors), he is every bit as incandescent and disappointed as he looks. The photograph was taken in 1907 during a visit by the mendacious Secretary of the Interior James R. Garfield, who had journeyed from Washington DC to persuade Charlo of the government's good will. Charlo had initially wanted to fight the white man to the end, and now he knew it was too late. He died three years later, his spirit broken. He wrote:

Since our forefathers first beheld him, [the white man] has filled graves with our bones ... His course is destruction. He spoils what the Spirit, who gave us this country, made beautiful and clean ... What is he? Who sent him here? We were happy when he first came ... Had heaven's Chief burnt him with some mark, we might have refused him. No, we did not refuse him in his weakness. In his poverty, we fed, we cherished him - yes, befriended him, and showed the fords and defiles of our lands ... We owe him nothing. He owes us more than he will pay ... His laws never gave us a blade of grass nor a tree nor a duck nor a grouse nor a trout.

The town of Charlo, Montana, is named in the chief's memory.

The white settlers didn't win because they were better people, but because they happened to have got hold of guns and horses at a crucial juncture. The Native Americans didn't lose because they were in any way deficient, but because they did not understand until it was too late the scale of the guile they were up against. Chief Charlo has every right to his rage.

X.
Industrialisation

Bill Brandt, *Northumberland Miner
at his Evening Meal*, 1937

People have always worked and always suffered doing so – but when we look at Bill Brandt's image of a Northumberland miner eating his supper, we know that we have entered a new stage in the history of labour and its attendant agonies.

It was the economist Adam Smith (1723–1790) who first proposed that the hallmark of the modern industrial system was specialisation. In the pre-industrial world, most people had done a bit of everything: sewing, carpentry, animal husbandry, baking ... It was hard, but there was variety. Then, in the late 18th century, it was realised how much more profitable work could be if most people devoted themselves exclusively to a single task. In the new factories of the Industrial Revolution, work grew at once punishingly intense – and exceptionally narrow.

The Northumberland miner was, at birth, ostensibly, a full participant in the story and possibilities of humanity, but part of the poignancy of his portrait stems from our recognition of the way that he has, in effect, been entirely subsumed by his labour. He is, above everything else, a miner: a man who toils for twelve hours a day in a dark tunnel so that trains can run and his overseers can buy themselves country houses and racehorses. That he has sat down to eat without scrubbing off the soot is a sign that he has – with weary resignation – accepted that he will never shake off his working persona; that he will never be cleansed of what the system has done to him. So, there is no point pretending that he could miraculously transform himself into a painter, a carefree father or a musician in the ten hours left to him before he is expected back at the mine. His wife doesn't protest at this sombre conclusion. She might have tried to keep another story going, but it seems kinder to stay true to the facts – and lay on a plentiful meal.

When Karl Marx (1818–1883) encouraged people to imagine life after capitalism had been overthrown, he talked principally about the possibilities of diversified lives:

In communist society ... nobody has one exclusive sphere of activity but each can become accomplished in any branch he wishes ... thus it is possible for me to do one thing today and another tomorrow, to hunt in the morning, to fish in the afternoon, rear cattle in the evening, criticise after dinner ... without ever becoming a hunter, fisherman, shepherd or critic.

The cruelty of capitalism stemmed, for Marx, not only from the way that we were expected to work very hard for low rewards. He also directed his anger at the way in which the industrial system forced us into specialised roles that curtailed the freedom of our minds. We become our work – which is why the first question we are asked by strangers is still 'What do you do?' Even if we are not crouching in a mine shaft, we typically have no choice but to gradually take on the personality of the job we perform. The police officer reduces themselves to an automaton of authority and discipline. The school teacher speaks to everyone as if they were their distracted charges in need of sharp instruction.

This may seem like an incidental critique of modern work, but it goes close to the heart of the injuries of labour. Whatever enlargements it can sometimes deliver to our personalities, our work possesses an extreme capacity to trammel our spirits. We may ask ourselves painfully what sort of people we might have been had we had the opportunity to do something different. There will be parts of us that we have had to kill (perhaps brutally), or that lie in shadow, twitching occasionally on Sunday afternoons or in the late hours.

As if mirroring the neglect of the coal-mining employers, tellingly, the photographer Bill Brandt (1904–1983) never recorded his sitter's name. We know him simply as the 'Northumberland miner'. But when we observe him as he eats, without grasping any of the particulars, we instinctively understand how much more of life and of himself this unfortunate man deserved to explore.

Negative by T. H. O'SULLIVAN.   Entered according to act of Congress, in the year 1865, by A. Gardner, in the Clerk's Office of the District Court of the District of Columbia.   Positive by A. GARDNER, 511 7th St., Washington.

Timothy H. O'Sullivan, *A Harvest
of Death, Gettysburg, Pennsylvania,
July 4, 1863*, 1863

2.

At the beginning of the industrial age, the noblest hope for the media was that it would manage to stir up, and usefully direct, the conscience of a distracted and forgetful public – and so help to bring about an end to partisanship, destruction and slaughter.

The implication was that we often end up supporting troubling causes in large part because we can't see their ultimate consequences: we lack the imagination to trace the connections between our positions and the ensuing, offstage problems like pollution, corruption, ugliness – and in extremis, impoverishment and death. We reward greed and cruelty because we can't picture the true costs of our allegiances.

With an optimistic vision of the power of the media, the first journalistic photographers of the 19th century therefore set out to catalogue the iniquities and horrors of their time – in order to shock their audiences into support for social reform, diplomacy and kindness. If, for example, war was popular, this could be only because its real nature was largely unknown: the average citizen had simply no clue what war really meant. They might, at best, have heard a few inaccurately heroic tales in a tavern or glimpsed a sanitised painting done years after a battle. Only now, thanks to photography, they would be able to contemplate the full tragedy from head on – and perhaps become pacifists at a stroke.

Timothy O'Sullivan (1840–1882) was an exceptionally brave and determined early photographer, who took great personal risks to show the public the realities of the American Civil War. He observed sharpshooters picking off troops; he placed himself within range of artillery fire; and, as soon as the battle of Gettysburg was over, he went out among the 51,000 dead (the highest number in any battle ever fought on American soil) and unflinchingly captured their stricken faces and bodies.

His images continue to appal; it becomes newly inconceivable how creatures who were once small children would do this to one another. The difficulty is that – in relation to its founding ambitions – O'Sullivan's work has been more or less in vain. No modern report on a war has, in truth, ever made a difference to its outcome. Art seems congenitally unable to rescue life.

And the culprits, as ever, are those twin devilish tendencies in our nature: inattention and forgetfulness. We know – at the moment when we look – why so much is wrong; but then we move on. Something else distracts us, we overlook our noble vows, we quickly forget what we were so incensed about only two hours ago. Clever governments and the powerful know that, in order to weaken people's resolve, they simply need to put out so much news, and create so much outrage, that everyone forgets what the real issues might be. An excess, rather than a censorship, of news is the only means required to weaken political will.

The greatest homage we might pay to O'Sullivan and the souls of those he helped us to see is, in a few days from now, to remember.

Philip James de Loutherbourg,
An Avalanche in the Alps, 1803

3.

It is – ostensibly – a very awful moment indeed. Three people were just about to cross a small wooden bridge across a ravine somewhere in the Alps when, from above, a vast mass of stone and rock cascaded down and almost swept them to their deaths. They look on in terror and surprise as, around them, the previously settled world takes on the chaotic and sombre appearance of a circle of Hell.

The painter, Philip James de Loutherbourg (1740–1812), had begun his career turning out peaceful bucolic scenes: cows in meadows, sunsets, quiet babbling brooks. Real success had only come to him when he shifted course to show us terror: fires, storms, shipwrecks, graveyards. It was scenes of ordinary life being subsumed and crushed that appeared properly to excite his audiences and that brought him wealth and renown.

Collective tastes in art tell us a lot about what a society happens to be missing in itself. We love qualities in images that somehow promise to return us to inner equilibrium and harmony. It is no surprise that, as the world became modern, efficient, rational and regimented, there were waves of enthusiasm for art that depicted life in long-distant times and atmospheres. Citizens in the vast cities of the Industrial Revolution hankered after pictures of Medieval courts, Pacific islands and ancient Greek and Roman temples. What we call 'beautiful' at any point are, in large part, works that contain wisdom or virtues we are in exile from.

We might then ask why de Loutherbourg met with such success with an avalanche – and why, along the way, a whole generation of artists in the 19th century thrived on painting the night sky, waterfalls, glaciers, furious seas and volcanic eruptions. An explanation is that the Industrial Revolution placed humanity in a new relationship to itself: thanks to the discoveries of science and the marshalling of energy in gigantic factories, humankind became immensely and apparently boundlessly powerful. Cities grew exponentially, machinery unleashed gargantuan wealth, mass communication generated a non-stop din of competitive chatter.

In the circumstances, what many began to crave was some way to relativise ourselves, reminders that we were not in reality as dauntingly all-powerful as we might appear. We longed to be made to feel small again by non-human forces, in order that we not feel so oppressed by the never-ending achievements of technology and the obsessions and social one-upmanship of urban life. We craved to be reminded – in order to lessen our sense of competitiveness, ambition and humiliation – of our ultimate nullity in the broader scheme of things.

Given the inordinate hours we spend fearing that we have not achieved enough, that our reputation is not sound, that we have failed to become the entrepreneurs or magnates we once dreamt of being, there isn't in reality horror, but in fact relief, in contemplating (from a safe vantage point) a landslide or a storm or a glacier. At last, now, we can – as a species – be put back in our place. What matter the differences between any two humans, given the gap between the mightiest human and the true scale, strength, age and mystery of the universe?

A real avalanche can be a deadly risk to Alpine travellers; it turns out to be an uncommonly useful tool of contemplation for fretful industrial moderns.

Positivist Temple to the Religion of
Humanity, Porto Alegre, Brazil, late
19th century

4

The most seismic development in the West in the 19th century arguably had little to do with urbanisation, democratisation or industrialisation. It was about God. Over the course of the century, in almost every European country, a majority went from trusting in, to questioning the existence of a higher being; it was the century when God died.

One of the more imaginative responses to this consequential loss came from French sociologist Auguste Comte (1798–1857). Comte did not believe that it was possible for a society to survive without the comforts and guidance of religion; there would be too much isolation, personal ambition and madness without it (he was prescient). At the same time, he appreciated that science had invalidated all traditional belief systems and hence that a new credo would have to be formulated. His answer to the conundrum was to mine existing religion, as well as psychology, art and philosophy, in order to launch a new secular religion that he termed 'a religion for humanity'.

Comte appreciated that all religions had owed a great deal of their impact to art and architecture. So he called for the construction of a network of 'temples to humanity'. They would be, in effect, highly attractive community centres that would draw on the talents of the best builders and painters of the day, and provide a focal point where adherents could gather every week and listen to talks and nurture friendships. Comte specified that above the west-facing stage, there should always be a sentence written in gold letters capturing the self-focused, yet also Classical, essence of his new philosophy: 'Connais toi pour t'améliorer' (Know yourself to improve yourself).

In two volumes outlining the contents of his religion, called *The Catechism of Positive Religion or Summary Exposition of the Universal Religion*, Comte announced that there should be twelve updated 'saints', great figures from politics, science and the arts (Descartes, Goethe and Voltaire among them) and that every month of the year should be dedicated to one of them, with members attending lectures and reading groups about their work.

In addition, Comte understood how much emotional guidance had been offered by religions and imagined a network of modernised priests, who would not try to save souls but would dispense useful advice on challenges like marriage, bringing up children, coping with illness and facing up to mortality. We can imagine them as early versions of psychotherapists.

Comte's plans were a mixed success. Though the press of the day mocked him as an eccentric, a devoted core rallied to the cause. Brazil, then a young country, was particularly interested in his programme and a number of temples to humanity were built in four Brazilian cities – where they survive to this day.

Some of Comte's plans were unfortunate. Against considerable opposition from his acolytes, Comte insisted that his girlfriend Clothilde should be venerated in every temple as the symbol of feminine wisdom. His modernised priests were meant to wear a medal around their necks bearing Comte's image – and their talks were to end with a homily to Comte: 'Great teacher and Master, revealer of Humanity, prophet of the future, founder of the one universal religion'. This was closer to the problematic sides of religion than might have been effective.

Whatever its shortcomings, Comte's 'religion for humanity' proved to be a highly suggestive and still relevant experiment – arguably the most relevant of the century. It accurately zeroed in on the need to provide a replacement for the key activities and concepts that had accompanied religions for most of human history, and sought to recast them for a fractured and restless secular world. It was a creative attempt to rescue some of what remains beautiful, touching, reasonable and wise from what no longer seems true. We might – in the manner of good historians – use this distinctive byway of the past to reimagine a less lonely and existentially puzzled future.

Baptistery of Saint John, Florence,
Italy, consecrated 1128 (19th-century
photograph)

5.

One of the leading ambitions of modern society has been to make life's pleasures and opportunities open to as many people as possible. 'Accessible' has become one of our greatest terms of praise, democracy is our highest political ideal and inclusivity can feel like our most urgent social aspiration. We retain – by contrast – nothing but contempt and anger for concepts like exclusive, aristocratic and elite.

But because there is always value in studying what is outlying and contrary, we can in the modern context usefully turn to the example of the French novelist, Marie-Henri Beyle (1783–1842), normally known by his pen-name Stendhal. He wrote two of the greatest novels of French literature, *Le Rouge et le Noir* and *La Chartreuse de Parme*. Born into a middle-class family in Grenoble, as a young man, Stendhal worked for the Napoleonic regime in minor diplomatic and military roles. After Bonaparte's exile, he grew disenchanted with his native country, which he associated with illiberalism, anger and cynicism. He knew plenty of people but had few real friends. In company, he had difficulty articulating his thoughtful, impish nature (the waspish critic Lytton Strachey once described him as combining the penetrating intelligence of a High Court judge with the soft heart and weepy nature of an 11-year-old girl).

Stendhal was no political reactionary. He wanted the vote to be open to all and for the talented to progress whatever their backgrounds. Nevertheless, he became drawn to the idea of an 'aristocracy': that is, of the existence of a distinguished elite who could be favoured above others. This had nothing whatsoever to do with an aristocracy of the blood. What Stendhal cared about was an aristocracy of the heart, an elite who knew how to feel, think, connect and be quiet and sad in ways that few seemed to savour. He believed that, though modern democratic society proclaimed the equality of all peoples and stridently sought to place everyone on the same footing, the reality was that only a narrow group would ever really understand matters in the profound, generous way he favoured.

Stendhal left France and served as French consul at Trieste and Civitavecchia. It was in Italy that he began to use a phrase with which we still associate him. He remarked, in letters and in his books, that he would dedicate his work and his life not to the masses, not to society in general, but to 'the happy few'. The phrase had come from Shakespeare (a line in *Henry V*: 'we few, we happy few, we band of brothers'), but Stendhal gave it his own meaning. He understood by it a minority of people, all of them his imaginary friends, who had the kind of sensibility he revered but which was out of step with modern times. Such people were emotionally sensitive, thoughtful, loved to be on their own, adored art and culture, hated political hysteria, were sexually generous and open and loved the sort of peaceful, aesthetically sensitive life that he had discovered in Italy. The 'happy few' could be recognised as those who had known unrequited love, were full of regrets about their career but couldn't abide the fierce tactics to succeed at it, were moved by Mozart, liked to laugh warmly at the tragedies of existence – and might well up with tears at a building like the Baptistery of Saint John in Florence. The Baptistery had especially touched Stendhal by its graceful symmetry, its beauty contrasting sharply with the chaos and ugliness of the world.

We often feel wretched for thinking that we don't like many people, that most of those we meet are disappointing and that we don't hold out much hope for the future of our species. It isn't fun to be misanthropic in a modern, excited democracy. Still, in dejected moods we can turn to Stendhal as our own imaginary friend who will never punish us for our reservations. We may not be misanthropes at all; we may just secretly, without having known it ourselves, have all along belonged to that narrow aristocracy of the heart: the happy few. Cynics are only idealists with awkwardly high standards. No wonder we have been so lonely – and how hopeful to think that we might not always have to be so.

XI.
Africa

Painting of a hippopotamus on
a flake of limestone, Egypt,
New Kingdom, c. 1479–1425 BCE

Ancient Egyptian philosophy was astute in its tendency to use animals to describe aspects of what we might term the psyche or the internal world. And few animals played a more significant role in this than the hippopotamus.

They became extinct in Egypt in the early part of the 19th century, but in the ancient period hippos had thrived in the waters of the Nile. Much of the time, they lay submerged, with only their backs visible – resembling a small island on which birds might sit – but, especially if they were disturbed, they might arise with tremendous force, blasting out water from their powerful nostrils, shaking off mud and weeds and terrifying onlookers. They were known for their vast appetites and could make their way through a whole field in one night (their favoured time for eating). In a bad mood, they could severely maim and on occasion kill people; to this day, they are responsible for more deaths in Africa than any other mammal.

These unusual, massive creatures fascinated the ancient Egyptians, who accorded them a central but (as we will see) twofold mythological identity and represented them continually in their art. On the one hand, hippos were associated with the god Seth, who stood for chaos, violence, disorder and force. It was Seth who was at work whenever war or fighting broke out, wherever there was dissent and tumult. It was then the task of the Pharaoh, who ruled in the name of Horus, god of kingship, order and law, to restore *maat* (justice and order). At certain times of the year, hippos would be specially captured for the Pharaoh and placed in an arena to be ritually killed, in a ceremony that symbolised the conquest of Horus over Seth.

However, the Egyptians also observed that hippos were intensely protective of their young (of whom they tended to have a very small number) and also that they were in the habit of roaring at both sunrise and sunset, which made it seem as though they might be responsible for helping the sun into the world every morning and settling it into the night at dusk. They were, on this basis, connected to the goddess Taweret, who looked after all matters of generation and fertility and played a special role in the protection of children and pregnant mothers. Few families were without some kind of sculpted amulet of Taweret, depicted as an upright hippo with large breasts, who would be prominently placed wherever children might be playing or sleeping.

We can conclude that, in the ancient Egyptian mind, the hippopotamus stood for a dual force, one that was at times destructive and ferocious, and at other points nurturing and beneficent. What counted was the correct management of the hippo-like aspects of the world, of nature and, viewed more psychologically, of the self. A person might allow the negative sides of their internal hippo to dominate their character, leading to unpredictability, meanness and destructiveness. Or, with sufficient piety, observance and will, they could tame the fierce animal – as Horus had overcome Seth – and use it to power acts of benevolence and affection. The same force that could smash a village might gently guard a defenceless infant during its afternoon nap, or an 8-month-pregnant first-time mother on her way to market.

To the ancient Egyptians, who were constantly on their guard against the consequences of a spiritually unbalanced world – or individual soul – *maat* mattered above anything else, and hippos were crucial to its maintenance. We don't have to be literal believers in the mythology of the hippo to appreciate what seemed to be at stake, nor to perceive that, even in our own times, our serenity and effectiveness may depend on ensuring that our internalised hippos, negative and positive, have been correctly subdued, harnessed and directed towards protecting what we most cherish.

Ifa divination tapper (*iroke Ifa*), Yoruba,
Owo region, Nigeria, 17th-18th century

2

The Yoruba people are an ethnic group, 35 million in number, who have, since the first millennium BCE, lived in what is now Nigeria and neighbouring Benin and Togo. For the psychologically minded, the Yoruba are especially rewarding to study because of their way of approaching mental troubles.

In Yoruba culture, those whose minds have been giving them difficulties have traditionally gone to visit a special figure called a *babalawo*. According to the Yoruba, mental troubles are almost always the result of trouble or discord in our relations with our dead ancestors, who inhabit an invisible – but active – spirit world called *orun*, as distinct from the tangible everyday realm, which is termed *aye*. In a spiritual consultation known as a *daf*, a *babalawo* will examine a sufferer's *ori* or mental state, which is determined by the interplay between past and present; only by sifting through and resolving the past can one's true potential (or *ori inu*) be released. As part of the healing process, the *babalawo* will make use of a highly prized object called an *iroke Ifa*, a divination tapper, which they start to beat rhythmically on the ground, while asking a sufferer to both describe their symptoms and connect these to any relatives who come to mind.

The sound of the *iroke* creates a special atmosphere that separates the session from the day to day – and helps to relax the sufferer and render them more responsive to the *babalawo's* interventions and advice. The striking sound is also intended to initiate a direct connection with the perturbing ancestors above. The tapper's design shows a solemn kneeling figure representing the sufferer, on top of whose head is carved a divine bird, with the power to fly into the *orun* and connect with the invisible dead.

The *babalawo* doesn't merely speak about a given ancestor with their client, they speak directly to them as a means of resolving the issues at play. Someone might – for example – arrive complaining of feeling like an impostor at work and of their tendency to sabotage their own best professional efforts. The *babalawo*

might suggest that their success in business might be threatening or humiliating to the long-dead father that the client described as an impressive but tyrannical figure. At which point the *babalawo* might do one of two things: either have a conversation with the father explaining that the offspring had every right to thrive and realise their *ori inu*. Or, if the father seemed resistant to argument and continued to appear vengeful, then the *babalawo* would firmly banish them deeper into the spirit world and forbid them from ever intervening again in the quotidian sphere of the *aye*.

Or someone might be suffering from a sense that a much-loved grandmother was lonely and unwell in the spirit world. The client might be beset by feelings of guilt, which would kick in whenever they tried to enjoy themselves with friends or with a partner. Here, too, the *babalawo* would call up the ancestor with their *iroke* and, together with the client, would personally explore how the relative was doing. The *babalawo* would encourage the client to say anything they wanted to the departed one, to offer words of comfort and then – ideally – to bid them a proper farewell, and put them into a deep and soothing sleep, newly reassured that their spirit could from now on rest more easily and leave the living undisturbed.

The Western world takes huge pride in the psychological intelligence that led to the emergence of psychotherapy. We don't need to denigrate the achievement behind this discipline to realise that much that was thought to have been discovered only in the modern age may, in reality, have been known about long ago, albeit in slightly different terms. We may even ourselves want to seek out a session or two with a *babalawo*, whose mystical authority and rhythmic sound might finally silence the more persistent of our ancestors, who have until now evaded the reach of Western therapy.

Detail from a Roman mosaic depicting
a merchant leading a camel train, from
Bosra, capital of the Roman province
of Arabia, Syria, 2nd century CE

3

Our concepts of art can sometimes lead us to neglect phenomena of beauty that fail to match certain familiar, but rigid, notions of aesthetic value. We may be so busy looking out for traditional works like paintings, sculptures or temples that we may walk right past other, equally deserving elements – like aqueducts, air traffic control systems or the layout of city streets. Thus we have neglected a practice which, by all fair measures, should merit a place in the pantheon of art: the Saharan camel train.

The tradition of carrying goods for great distances on long columns of camels flourished between the 6th and the 16th centuries CE in the deserts of North Africa. Camel trains were run by Berber tribes from what is now southern Morocco and Algeria, and provided the chief trade route between the Mediterranean and the wealthy empires of sub-Saharan Africa, like those of Mali and Songhai. The trains were wondrous at a number of levels.

Firstly, there was the camel itself, a creature of unusual refinement, with its long, thick eyelashes, its unhurried, lolling gait and amused-seeming, sympathetic expression. The dromedary was perfectly adapted to its unfeasibly arduous circumstances, able to carry up to 400 kilograms for 40 kilometres a day, raise its body temperature to 41° Celsius without sweating, and go for several weeks without drinking – before eventually, at famous oases like those at Bilmer in north-eastern Niger, taking in more than 100 litres in ten minutes.

A caravan might comprise as many as 3,000 camels, collectively bearing the equivalent of thirty-five modern shipping containers full of goods. It took between forty and sixty days to cross the Sahara, an expanse of 9 million square kilometres, larger than the next three deserts (the Gobi, the Arabian and the Australian deserts) combined. Typically, caravans heading south would be carrying salt, pottery, lamps, cloth, glassware, perfume bottles, copper ingots, dates and raisins – while those heading north would be bearing animal hides, gold, ivory, ostrich feathers, kola nuts and tobacco.

Runners were employed to go ahead of the main caravan and fetch water from upcoming oases, as well as prepare their merchants for business. Palm-fringed settlements like Oualata and Tamentit grew wealthy and architecturally distinguished on the back of the camel trains – and sprang into life as the animals appeared across the gilded horizon.

A camel train was led by a highly trained and experienced figure called a *khabir*. *Khabirs* had a minute understanding of geography and economics; they knew how to use the stars to navigate the sand dunes, how to negotiate in multiple languages, how to deal with snake and scorpion bites, and how to win over local tribesmen (they often made strategic marriages in oases along their routes). They were also figures of religious authority, expected to lead daily prayers and provide spiritual counsel.

Many were talented storytellers, too. Trains generally started walking at dawn, rising to the sound of horns and kettle drums, but stopped in the midday heat under burgundy-coloured tents for dates and honey, yogurt and pistachio drinks. In the idle hours, a *khabir* might reinforce morale through tales of valour, or move the spirit with songs of love, separation and longing. The men could look up at the stars in the cool night and feel themselves close to divinity.

Gradually, over the 16th century, Saharan overland trade was eclipsed by fast Portuguese ships travelling along the African coast. The oases fell into disrepair and the camel trains were disbanded. Life would have been difficult on the trains, but stories of them may nevertheless deeply touch those among us who dream of a nomadic existence under a boundless sky to alleviate our sense of melancholy and constriction. We might not have to think very long if a *khabir* were magically to invite us to drop everything and accompany them, and a thousand dromedaries, across the dunes, from Tindouf to Gao, with a consignment of dates, olives and incense.

The Berlin conference, 1884. Wood
engraving after a drawing by Adalbert
von Rößler, from a late 19th century
edition of 'Illustrierte Zeitung'

4

By the start of the 21st century, Africa was the poorest continent on Earth, its countries at the bottom of all indexes for development, health, welfare and freedom. Per capita income had either stagnated or, in some cases, fallen over decades. Half of the continent's population lived on less than a dollar a day; between 1981 and 2002, the number of its people in poverty doubled, and its food production fell by 10 percent.

The immediate cause was conflict. A high share of African nations had been either at war with one another or with themselves since independence. The explanation for this had nothing to do with entrenched belligerence or querulousness: it lay squarely with a too-often-forgotten conference organised by the German chancellor, Otto von Bismarck, in Berlin in 1884.

In the Reich Chancellery, a gigantic map was put up on the wall, showing Africa's natural features, but leaving out all place names, let alone references to ethnic groups, religions or languages. Over three months, delegates from the main European powers haggled and bartered over gold mines and plantations, copper deposits and forests, in a landscape that they cynically pretended was virgin territory. They then took out their rulers, drew straight lines on the map and created nations. Not a single African was invited to the meeting.

The new countries that emerged from this delusional process destroyed any possibility of a sense of belonging or patriotism. They were arbitrarily made-up places, designed to suit European priorities, and they pushed together ethnic groups that, over centuries, had had nothing to do with one another, spoke different languages, believed in different religions and experienced long histories of rivalry and suspicion. It was as if someone had summarily created a new country out of a bit of Greece, a slice of Germany and a swathe of Finland – and then wondered why things didn't work out well.

Many of the countries we know in Africa today did not exist before this brutal partitioning: there was no such territory as 'Nigeria' or 'Mali', 'Namibia' or 'Gabon'. The borders of modern Burkina Faso cut across territory that traditionally belonged to twenty-one different cultural and linguistic groups. The Ewe people, who have a 500-year history, were divided between present-day Ghana and Togo. In the horn of Africa, the Europeans split the Somali people between French Somaliland, British Somaliland and Italian Somaliland (now Somalia and Somaliland) and provinces of Ethiopia and northern Kenya. The Afar people of Ethiopia were partitioned into modern Ethiopia, Eritrea and Djibouti, and the Anyuaa and Nuer were scattered between Ethiopia and what is now the Republic of South Sudan.

A simple rule of thumb when trying to determine the difficulties an African country will face is to take a look at how straight its borders are. The straighter they happen to be, the more likely it is that the Europeans in Berlin drew a line through existing tribes or kingdoms – and the result will be chaos and civil war. The more wiggly they are, the more likely it is that an old tribal arrangement was accidentally respected and, therefore, that the country could be a little more internally stable and cohesive. Botswana, the richest, least corrupt and most democratic country in Africa, has wiggly borders on three of its four sides and is home to just one ethnic group, the Tswanas, who have lived within the modern nation's borders for many centuries. By contrast, Equatorial Guinea, which has only straight lines and a majority ethnic group, the Fangs, who are divided up across three countries, has been in strife for decades.

We are reminded of the importance of kinship in the maintenance of peace. Nations require more than flags and anthems to hold them together; they depend on a long-standing sense of belonging and a shared identity to ensure cohesion and a sense of trust. Europeans made a catalogue of mistakes in Africa: one of their very greatest was to forget what a country is.

Kenneth Scott Associates, Dr Easmon
Residence, Accra, Ghana, 1959

5

One of the difficulties African countries have faced since their independence is that solutions to their varied challenges have largely been developed outside their borders and imposed on them without respect for their distinctive cultures and contexts. Ideas that might have worked well in Washington DC or Paris have proved less effective in N'Djamena or Bangui. African nations have struggled to find a version of modernity attuned to their uniqueness.

An inspiring model of how a reconciliation between Western modernity and localism might function can be found in an area too often left out of political consideration: architecture. During the colonial period, much of civic architecture in Africa was profoundly unsuited to its environment. Its examples were ornate, bombastic, designed to impress and intimidate: a stifling version of neo-Palladianism in the tropics.

By the middle of the 20th century, there emerged in many countries – particularly in equatorial Africa – a generation of architects who wanted to do better. They were familiar with the history of their own vernacular architecture: they knew about rammed earth construction, wind towers, stilts, louvres, communal halls and thatched roofs. But they had also had their eyes opened to Western techniques. They had heard the theories of Le Corbusier and Mies van der Rohe, and understood the opportunities afforded by concrete and glass, open-plan designs and prefabrication techniques.

Their dream was of a synthesis. The earliest successful example came with Abidjan's City Hall, built in 1956. Raised on pilotis (piers or stilts), it was constructed out of bush-hammered concrete, with panels decorated with local ochre quartz pebbles and wooden shutters painted with designs of Akan masks. The hall appeared to whisper that one could be true to the history of the Ivory Coast while drawing amply on the benefits of Western modernism. It was only fitting that the country's first president, Félix Houphouët-Boigny, decided to proclaim independence in the building's main courtyard in August 1960.

In neighbouring Ghana, in the town of Kumasi, Kwame Nkrumah University of Science and Technology was inaugurated in 1961, and named after the country's first prime minister. With cross ventilation in its roofs, and a layout that drew on that of a traditiona Ashanti village, it, too, contributed to an emerging African modernism. It was hoped that this would be the MIT or Harvard of the region and help Africa patent its first drugs.

Perhaps the most inspiring example of the new modernism came in the form of an ordinary house commissioned by a private citizen in Accra, Dr Easmon, the first Ghanaian heart surgeon (described as 'the father of cardiac surgery in West Africa') in 1959. Raised 2.4 metres off the ground, with windows protected by large shutters positioned only on its north and south façades, the house perfectly understood its location. It required no air conditioning and yet had the openness and flexibility of the best European Modernist villas. Its elegant rooms were an apt setting for a collection of local Ghanaian art. It spoke of a life governed by order, intellectual depth, kindness and fellow feeling.

We know what a good future for Africa will be like, for its form is already legible in examples of outstanding contemporary architecture. The hope is that the complicated world around them will, in time, align ever more closely with their message of enlightenment and harmonised progress.

Stuart Franklin, *Lobby of the Gaweye
Hotel, Niamey, Niger, 2005*

6

From mid-morning in the best hotels of Niamey, Niger's capital, the bosses, government officials, middlemen, traders and fixers take their places in large armchairs in the lobbies and meeting rooms. Their hushed voices create a steady murmur, occasionally interrupted by a loud enquiry at the concierge desk or a commotion in the traffic-choked streets outside. Despite decades of effort by NGOs and – at points – parts of the government, it is evident that at least some of the transactions being negotiated over coffee will fall outside of a standard understanding of legality. The French language has twisted itself delicately around the matter. One carefully makes reference to a need for some *poivre* (pepper) or *une petite envelope* (a small envelope); a deal might be done if one can *attacher la chèvre* (tie the goat) or *faire boire à quelqu'un* (give somebody a drink).

It sounds dismal, but that it happens on such a large scale suggests that we are dealing with something more than individual moral weakness; we are faced with congenital incentives to game the system. The Polish journalist Ryszard Kapuściński (1932–2007) – who spent the greater part of his career in Africa – remarked that, in most African countries, the first thing anyone appointed to a position of wealth and authority will do is invite their extended family to join them in their good fortune. Soon they will have given their brother a job, made sure their sister is looked after, put their father-in-law up for a contract and made certain that their cousin's wife's uncle has been armed with a fulsome letter of recommendation.

They aren't doing this out of venality, or a committed desire to do down their business or the state, but simply because it is expected of them. It is, in certain places, considered just as mandatory to help out family at the expense of any other consideration as – in other places – it is critical to keep private interests outside of work. There are countries where it might be as important to promote a not-necessarily-qualified uncle as it is in others to ensure that a job is open to an array of candidates without ties of blood and marriage to the employer. It is, to push the argument, in some places as dishonest not to favour kinfolk as it is in other places wholly corrupt to do so.

Hence the relative futility – despite so much energetic moralism – of attempts to 'clean up' politics or business in many African nations. They are only 'dirty' if one approaches the matter from the point of view of a German civil servant or an American law professor. It can never work to label as corrupt practices that are underwritten by the established method of functioning of an entire society. One cannot partially institute a meritocracy in a land dominated by a clan system of preferment. There is no incentive for an individual patron to distribute advantages in a new way – according to someone's exam results or their years of professional experience – when, in every other walk of life, they will be penalised for doing so: shunned by those they care about, and ignored and ridiculed when they are themselves next in need and petitioning others for help.

A transparent, meritocratic system – of course – offers an entire society the greatest possible benefits, allowing talent to flourish and reducing the costs to any one person of being outside of kinship structures. However, in any immediate dynamic, for an individual, it will never make sense to break the mould and distribute their favours in the way that is customary in San Francisco or Zurich.

In the long term, what is happening at the sofas of Niamey's hotels won't be doing Niger (or any other nation) any good, but as the economist John Maynard Keynes bathetically observed, in the long term we are all dead. And in the meantime, to our 'uncle' in the lobby of the Gaweye Hotel, there is a niece to be housed, a brother-in-law to be helped through exams, and a great-aunt's grandson in urgent need of a little 'whisky' in the form of a five-year preferential contract in the uranium business. As they say around here with an apologetic shrug, *une chèvre doit brouter là ou elle est attachée* (a goat has to graze where it is tied).

XII.
Modernity

Walker Evans, *Subway Portrait,*
New York, 1938

1.

This is not exactly our line or our stop – but we are recognisably in the modern age, and in more or less our own times. The clothes have changed a bit and the carriages too (no moulded plastic and aluminium here, still the steel and wood construction of the past) but we can imagine the smell (the familiar mixture of creosote, brakes, dust and sweat), the sighs and whistles, the rattling, the way the lights dim at certain moments and the odd silence in the carriage itself. Everyone is looking aside, self-contained and elsewhere (except for perhaps a child, glancing around avidly, trying to make sense of an advert for dentures or anti-baldness cream above the head of someone their mother tells them not to stare at). If we were to get on board, we'd know just what we had to do.

How far we have come. The journey began shortly after the creation of the Earth. The carriage was empty save for the odd flying squirrel and restless grunting diplodocus. There were long periods of darkness, some explosions, a few rats and a duck-billed platypus, then the first humans got on, surprised to have made it, scared, vigilant and unwashed. Through the blackened windows, we saw pyramids, gladiator shows, cathedrals, gilded state rooms, cannons, ships of exploration, steam engines, telegraph poles. And then came the Broadway line and our two friends, he gets on at Canal Street, she at Union Square.

Walker Evans (1903–1975) was waiting for them, with a 35mm Contax hidden in his jacket, and a cable threaded down his sleeve so he could press the shutter without drawing attention to himself. He did it tirelessly between 1938 and 1941, crisscrossing the city on its main lines. There were over a thousand negatives; this is perhaps his best. It raises a set of questions for us: *What is this curious unholy modern world we have built? Where are we headed? What is the point?*

Evans' image is, above anything else, a picture of loneliness. We have built a world of appalling isolation. The two passengers are next to each other, but they are in different universes.

Through layers of gabardine and fur, they can intimate the presence of each other's arms, but every effort will be going into pretending that the other does not exist, was never a baby, does not have parents, isn't scared and won't have to die. It's how things are done, and yet how much love and curiosity we might have to give, how much we would be ready to help – if only these things were allowed.

She has lost the will to speak directly but she is beseeching us nevertheless: *I am exhausted, it can't go on much longer.* Because this is a work of art, we can meet her gaze and feel for her, in a way that we wouldn't for a real passenger. We both take art very seriously (this photograph hangs in the Metropolitan Museum of Art); and don't, in essence, give a shit.

Other than fear and shyness, what is separating us in the dark tunnels of modernity is, surprisingly but presciently, the newspaper: *Pal tells how gungirl killed.* The papers wouldn't put it exactly that way now, but the gist is unchanged. It wasn't necessarily clear, when this media tool came to maturity in the late 19th century, that it would end up devastating our minds. Almost everything that had been achieved through ink and paper until then had been about trying to reach the truth and put some good into the world. By contrast, this – unashamedly – was about creating envy, misplaced desire, outrage and hard-heartedness. Most of those whose names end up splashed in newspapers are mentally ill, not bad or perverted. We should collectively be running a hospital – but seem instead to be obsessed with running a prison, through whose bars everyone can gawp to try to feel better about their own restricted and compromised lives.

The picture isn't a political manifesto, but it prompts us, through its quiet sadness, to think of the stations that we might ideally want to be travelling to on the line of history: stations with greater colour, friendship, light and kindness – deliberately naive-sounding ingredients that may, nevertheless, be the bedrocks of the more humane future we long to reach.

Henri de Toulouse-Lautrec,
Au lit: le baiser, 1892

Two women are on a bed kissing: one looks considerably older than the other. They both have boyishly cut short hair. They might have been waiting a long time to do this. They aren't necessarily classically beautiful; the one on top appears thoughtful and kindly, perhaps always inclined to reflect on the impact of her actions on others. There is a strong sexual energy and explicitness to the scene, but above all, there is tenderness. We imagine – fairly but without evidence – that they are very much in love.

What sticks out is just how much needed to happen before this could take place – the kiss itself, but also its artistic representation, and then the picture's ensuing acclaim and popularity. For most of human history, in almost every country, a love between two women was either banned, heavily censored, or the subject solely of prurient pornographic interest. That two women might care for one another, that their feelings could have an explicit physical component but a large psychological one as well, that they might want to live together and perhaps marry, none of it was obvious. Just as frowned upon was the fact that there might be a large age gap between them.

Henri de Toulouse-Lautrec (1864–1901) was a French aristocrat who knew what it was like to stand far outside society's established norms. His parents had divorced when he was a boy, and he was looked after by a nanny whom he adored more than he ever did his mother. His father was a distant, punishing figure. A genetic defect meant that he never grew very much. He measured 1.52 metres and looked particularly unusual by virtue of having an adult-like torso and spindly child's legs; he was said to have had enlarged or hypertrophied genitals as well. As a result of his physical condition, he felt perpetually unacceptable. He couldn't marry, and conducted his intimate life almost entirely with prostitutes. It wasn't a coincidence that one of his best friends was that other internal exile and pilgrim, Vincent van Gogh. And another was Oscar Wilde – in the years after his downfall and disgrace. This was an artist who knew only too well what it meant to live on the other side of public approval.

At the heart of Toulouse-Lautrec's work is an invitation to stretch our conception of normality. It presents with grace and love what his world condemned as immoral and heinous. We think we have caught up with Toulouse-Lautrec's vision – but that may be our greatest sin. We pride ourselves on welcoming same-sex couples. We have the gall to think of ourselves as liberated. But we remain collectively as prejudiced and sealed off from genuine tolerance as the worst, most blinkered bourgeois of Toulouse-Lautrec's era. Whenever cases come to us without the protective veneer of overt public approval, we quickly sink back into the spite and judgementalness that we otherwise condemn in our ancestors.

There is plenty that we remain categorically opposed to. They may be different things these days, but they are things we unthinkingly abominate nevertheless: relationships between consenting adults with age gaps (that hasn't changed or has even worsened), people who have unfashionable political views, 'reprobates' who may not think the same as everyone else about class, money, gender, sport, children, media . . . We wouldn't hesitate to tie any of them to the stake. The subjects of our tolerance may have changed, but the predominance of intolerance has not.

We may have learnt to feel welcoming and gentle towards the two women in Toulouse-Lautrec's masterpiece. It's an achievement of sorts – and it has taken a few millennia. Still, we shouldn't imagine that a modern-day Toulouse-Lautrec – the wealthy son of divorced parents who loved his nanny and connected mostly with working-class women – would be at peace with very much in our own times. The battle against meanness is ongoing; and is never quite as necessary as when people start to delude themselves that they are enlightened.

Edward Burtynsky, *Oil Refineries #23*
(Oakville, Ontario), Canada, 1999

3

One of the distinguishing features of the modern world is that we generally have little clue as to how any of it really works. The old world may have offered us far less to buy, to visit and to benefit from, but it granted us the incidental gift of a hugely more secure hold on its functioning. We knew the origins of most of what we used and owned: we understood how houses were built (we might have put one up ourselves), what jobs involved and where our bread and meat came from. Though our learning wasn't always robust and relied heavily on mysticism and make-believe, we could even claim a sense of how the universe came into being, why we existed and what life was for.

We moderns have been denied any such clarity. We are surrounded by the most astonishing gadgets and have access to powers that the greatest kings of old could not have dreamt of. Yet we are also ignorant of so much, in a way that lends us a background impression of alienation and impotence. We have no clue how our phones work, what physicists and astronomers are really telling us, who made most of what we eat or what goes on with cables under the pavements. We don't understand the financial system or the mechanics of government. It's still puzzling how aeroplanes fly and satellites operate. As for the ultimate mysteries, it's wholly opaque what we might be doing in the universe, why we got going in the first place or why anything that is, really is.

Edward Burtynsky (b. 1955) seems to feel sympathy for our puzzlement. It's been his mission to take us to some of the places we are generally shielded from: the bits of the world that are hidden from us by manufacturers and civic authorities afraid of our curiosity. He takes the back off the television, as it were. We see factories, mines, quarries – and in a series that occupied him for years, oil refineries. Many of these last are of astonishing complexity and incidental beauty: dazzlingly polished pipes run everywhere, suggesting an underlying order and precision that speak of intelligence and care. We don't know in detail what is really going on, but we can be grateful to Burtynsky for bringing us here. The world of energy starts to feel a little less opaque. We have been given a right to wonder.

There could be so much further to go. We might want to see the revenue offices where our income tax is processed, the laboratories where our blood samples are analysed, the civil servants who decide on our curricula, or the managers responsible for keeping the lights on …

It would require art, in the sense of thought and aesthetic arrangement. What a feat, though, to make us feel how gripping finance or manufacturing really are, or to help us understand our position in space. Instead, our energies are powerfully diverted to 'entertainment', as though we were small children to be shielded from the truth with sentimental light shows. On a plane, we're encouraged to pull down the blinds and settle into films about lovestruck couples – even as, outside, two giant Rolls Royce Trent 1000 engines may be powering us at 700 kilometres an hour over the Andaman Sea while a first officer sends a string of coded electronic messages through the heavens to a control tower in Bangkok in a way that might as well be magic, for all that we understand of what's going on. Our handle on our fundamental situation is far shakier than that of a Medieval ancestor who had no access to a library and leant on explanations of demons and goblins. We have fallen back to relating in an essentially supernatural way to a human-built world that has spun out of our control.

If this matters, it is ultimately because we may want to change things – and we won't be able to unless we know more of how they are presently arranged; and, even more importantly, if we lack the mindset to feel that we have the right to strip away at apparent mysteries and refuse the numb and unquestioning manner we've been encouraged to adopt. The refinery is an emblem of where we might need to go more regularly and of the many pipes we should follow back to their source – so as to feel at home in a world we have been thrown into.

Martin Parr, *Benidorm,*
Spain, 2014

4

There are moods in which we may wonder, contemplating the froth, excitements and debris of modern civilisation, whether it has – in the end – all been worth it. Certainly, our achievements are dazzling – viewed from a particular angle. So many bright lights, Ferris wheels, Asian-themed restaurants, pay-as-you-go cards, ice cream parlours, flip-flops, paintball games and water parks. There is so much of 'us' everywhere, this noisy, self-confident, fussy, cantankerous species, with our hair curlers, diet books, anti-impotence pills, therapists, plans for success, childhood traumas and moisturisers. What an impression we must make, how incessant and unconcerned we are.

In a different mood, we might stand back – and doubt. Martin Parr appears to have done as much. He has gone with his camera to Benidorm, Europe's original fun palace, built on the orders of General Franco on a deserted bit of beach on the Costa Blanca, and looked at us wading like unhappy buffalo into the sun-cream-clotted waters of the Mediterranean. Some of us are still slim and hopeful, but many more of us are heavy, sun-burnt and confused. The little ones are shrieking with joy – but it might as well be terror, as though they were giving voice to our own existential agonies.

Along the seashore, an array of self-confident apartment buildings have been marshalled to attention, each one of them built to maximise their views while ruining everyone else's. So much intelligence has been devoted to producing this sort of locale and its mid-August high points. Hydraulic engineers, property surveyors, concrete consultants, salmonella disinfectant manufacturers, telecoms specialists, aeronautical technicians, motorway construction crews ... They have for decades collaborated to build a fitting centre of respite and joy – but we can wonder how much of their work has really scratched at the misery that ails us in the early hours.

Sitting under a parasol in the pitiless heat, we might suspect that much of the modern world has been built on a misunderstanding of what human beings really need to be content. Certainly we don't want the pharmacies and *pastelerías* to have empty shelves, and it is a distinct pleasure to be able to travel away from home on occasion to take in some olives and a sparkling water to the sound of 'Mamma Mia' on a terrace of the Pizzeria Avanti. Yet we can question the order of our priorities and the true cost of our advantages.

Was it, in the end, necessary to destroy every piece of coast from here to Cartagena, to build quite so high, to make so many people rich so that they might expend their fortunes as they have? And was it worth the price, along the way, to isolate everyone into narrow concrete cells, to set up such a frenetic system of rewards, to plant so few trees and to leave so little emphasis on sitting quietly, on deepening friendships and on appreciating the natural phenomena that surpass us?

'Civilisation is a hopeless race to discover remedies for the evils it produces', Jean-Jacques Rousseau realised back in 1770. There may be few better places to mull over such a misanthropic reflection – while feeling intermittently superior, tearful and absurd – than on a sun lounger at the Hotel Don Pancho on the beachfront in Benidorm.

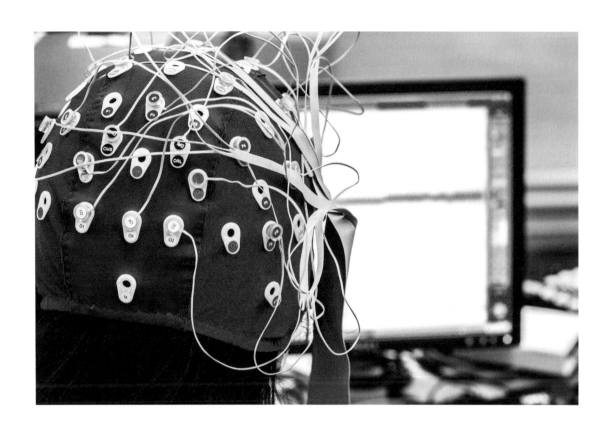

An electroencephalography or EEG cap,
London, 2021

5.

If historians have any conceivable skills as futurologists, it lies in their ability to step back from the day to day and discern patterns in the long-term past that may give an indication as to the likely future.

What the human animal has essentially always sought is increased mastery over its circumstances, in order to reduce its dependence on fate and improve access to its own satisfactions, chief and ultimate among these being life itself. Such a motive lies behind a range of history's long-term trends: the fight to ensure an adequate food supply, the development of tools and machinery, our journeys of exploration and our attempts at state-building and conquest.

The greatest gains have, in these areas, arguably already been made. We won't be stumbling on new (to us) continents again. All the same, the motives that drove us on continue to operate – and will find new arenas in which to expend themselves. Three in particular suggest themselves.

1. The mind
Neuroscience will be to the future what seafaring was to the 15th century, engineering to the 19th, and astrodynamics to the 20th: a field of knowledge that will give humans awesome new degrees of control over their circumstances. Present neuroscience will, within 200 years, look as pitiful as Renaissance medicine. We will eventually work out ways of allowing people to use the full contents of their own minds. Most of us currently die with only a fraction of our minds explored. Our greatest decisions are taken on a shamefully slender basis of self-understanding. We can't work out what we want or are capable of – and so repeatedly make grave mistakes, especially around our relationships, careers and, at a collective level, methods of governance. The brain scanners of the future will help us to bring our best thoughts to the surface: we will be able to be as clever as we can be. Only a fraction of people who have ever lived have made any substantial contribution to humanity: with better tools, billions of brains will attain their actual capacities. What we have called 'education', a fitful and haphazard process, will be transformed: we will pick up the best of what has been said and thought in minutes rather than decades. There will, as a result, be a good deal less debate and fruitless conjecture. The reasonable path on many topics will be clearer for all to see.

2. Offspring
A high percentage of individual and group activities have unconsciously been about the quest to optimise reproductive success. This is what has underpinned our obsessions with power, beauty, money and status. In future there will be another way to get to the same goal: we will learn how to manipulate the DNA of the next generation in order to create humans who are as clever, healthy and attractive as we have – in secrecy – always sought for them to be.

3. Death
Much of history has been about the desire to ward off death. We will, with time, finally understand the mechanics of cell degeneration – and reverse it. There may, one day, be humans who can legitimately expect never to die.

The sum total of these three changes will mean that, in effect, we will have created a new species. Archaic humans were around for 2 million years before *Homo sapiens* developed. There have been some seven varieties of us and (at 200,000 years old) we are the youngest. It is contrary to the principles of evolution to imagine that there wouldn't be an eighth, a bit like us but – to return to our theme – possessed of vastly greater powers of control.

Any number of shocking alternative scenarios are, of course, possible. This is simply one (inevitably) pitiful attempt to daydream about what might occur if humans keep doing what they have tended to do whenever they have been undistracted by the worst kinds of fear and folly.

Hubble Ultra Deep Field (HUDF),
the deepest image of the universe
ever taken, composited from
Hubble Space Telescope data, taken
between 24th September 2003 and
16th January 2004

6.

We can't know a lot about what lies ahead of us: the coming few billion years are somewhat murky. Oddly, however, we can with an astonishing degree of certainty know what will be coming to us at the very end. The conclusion to history is – already today – definitively clear, and, in a sense, very sad. Yet also, in a minor way, it is redemptively and profoundly comedic.

The sun formed 4.5 billion years ago, some 40 million years before the Earth. While it appears stable, it is in truth working its way through a limited supply of hydrogen and helium at its core. The more it does so, the more its heat will increase: 3.5 billion years from now, the sun will be 40 percent brighter than it is today, which will be enough to cause devastation on Earth: all the oceans will boil away, the atmosphere will evaporate into space, the ice caps will melt and the surface of the planet will be a molten toxic wasteland resembling Venus. Nothing – not the tiniest earthworm or parasite – will survive.

If this is not challenging enough (and the thought doesn't get as much attention as it should), 5.4 billion years from now, the sun will begin its endgame. It will enter its infamous red giant phase wherein, with the hydrogen in its core exhausted, it will expand exponentially, encompass the orbit of Mercury and Venus and then collide with the Earth, engulfing it and reducing it to nothingness. For about a billion more years, the murderous sun will burn as a red giant, then the hydrogen in its outer core will completely run out, and it will shrink into a fusion-less white dwarf giving off a pale glow of ionised gas before eventually, after 10 billion years, further collapsing into a stellar remnant known as a black dwarf – and then our part of the universe will be still, dark and eerie, and as if nothing had ever been.

We know – in theory – that we have a lot of time still ahead of us. The human story has only been going 200,000 years. It's been not much more than 4,000 years since King Sargon of Akkad established the world's first empire in Mesopotamia. We have – by most measures – an extraordinary amount of time left: 3.5 billion years ago, the very first living things, microbes called stromatolites, were only just coming into being, and the whole of history lay ahead of us. There is no hurry.

Nevertheless, the definiteness of the end is galling. Nothing that humanity does or cares about on the planet will endure. Everything will go. The Great Pyramid of Giza, the Golden Pavilion in Kyoto, the top-floor bedrooms in Paris' Le Meurice Hotel, the ice cream at the Gelateria Duse da Giovanni in Rome, the Atlantis bookshop in Santorini, the little red train that connects Chur with Silvaplana, the white sands of Kuramathi's beach in the Maldives, the paintings of Vilhelm Hammershøi, François Truffaut's *L'Argent de Poche*, the afternoon tea at the Sir Stamford in Sydney, every Madonna Bellini ever painted, the ceiling of King's College, Cambridge and the final movement of Bach's Mass in B Minor – all will be lost as the Earth prepares to boil for a few hundred million years at an intolerable 2,130°C.

It is inestimably depressing. And also, in a curious way, close to funny. If this is truly what is destined to happen, then everything that agitates us is absurd beyond measure. Every problem we have ever faced – our careers, relationships, reputations, regrets and failures – all are as naught in the face of the planet's eventual and inevitable complete evisceration.

We should use every measure we can to drain the present moment of its mock, crushing sense of significance. We have been granted an extraordinarily rich past to look back upon, a very long future to anticipate and, eventually, a very certain end point to resign ourselves to. We don't need to worry very much at all; as it turns out, we need only to love, to appreciate, to be kind and to learn – and always keep in mind our beautifully minuscule position in the prolonged, but blessedly finite, history of time.

List of Illustrations

p. 46   The geological clock: a projection of Earth's 4.5 Ga history on a clock ("Ma" = a million years (Megayear) ago; "Ga" = a billion years (Gigayear) ago). Artwork by Woudloper (Woodwalker) / Wikimedia Commons / Public Domain

p. 48   The Bornean orangutan (*Pongo pygmaeus*), Borneo. Photo © Aprison. Aprison / Dreamstime.com

p. 50   Fennec fox (*Vulpes zerda*). Photo © Wrangel / Dreamstime.com

p. 52   Median section of the brain. Lithograph by A. Leroux, after a drawing by N. H. Jacob. From the third volume of *Traité complet de l'anatomie de l'homme…* by Jean Marc Bourgery (Paris : L. Guérin, 1866-1867).

p. 54   Garry Winogrand, *New York*, 1961. © The Estate of Garry Winogrand, courtesy Fraenkel Gallery, San Francisco, CA, USA

p. 56   Christopher Columbus arrives in America. Engraving by Theodor de Bry from *Collected travels in the east Indies and west Indies* (*Collectiones peregrinationum in Indiam occidentalem*), vol. 4: Girolamo Benzoni, *Americae pars quarta. Sive, Insignis & admiranda historia de primera occidentali India à Christophoro Columbo* (Frankfurt, 1594). Rijksmuseum, Amsterdam, the Netherlands

p. 60   Marcel-Noël Lambert, *Acropole d'Athènes*, 1877. Watercolour, Indian ink, and graphite on paper, 200 × 312 cm. École nationale supérieure des Beaux-Arts (ENSBA), Paris, France. Photo © RMN-Grand Palais / Dist. Photo Scala, Florence

p. 62   *Aphrodite of Cnidus*. Marble, 1st-2nd century CE. Roman copy of a Greek original by Praxiteles, 4th century BCE. Museo Nazionale Romano (Palazzo Altemps), Rome, Italy. Photo © Marie-Lan Nguyen / Wikimedia Commons

p. 64   *The Lancellotti Discobolus*. Marble, 2nd century CE. Roman copy of a Greek bronze original by Myron, 5th century BCE. Palazzo Massimo alle Terme, Rome, Italy. Photo Eric Vandeville / akg-images

p. 66   The Antimenes Painter, black-figure amphora featuring a painting of olive-gathering, Attica, Greece, 520 BCE. Height 40.6 cm. British Museum, London, UK. Photo © The Trustees of the British Museum

p. 68   Odysseus and the Sirens, detail from a mosaic depicting scenes from Homer's *Odyssey*, 'House of Ulysses', Dougga, Tunisia. Roman, 3rd century CE. Musée national du Bardo, Tunis. Photo G. Dagli Orti / DeAgostini

p. 70   Jan Brueghel the Elder, *A Fantastic Cave with Odysseus and Calypso*, 1616. Oil on canvas. Private Collection. Photo Johnny Van Haeften Ltd., London / Bridgeman Images

p. 72   (left) The Apollo of the Belvedere. Marble, c. 120-140 CE. Roman copy of a lost bronze original by Leochares, second half of the 4th century BCE. Museo Pio-Clementino, Vatican, Italy. Photo © Jonghyunkim / Dreamstime.com

p. 72   (right) The young Bacchus with a personification of the vine (Ampelus). Marble, Roman, c. 150-200 BCE. Height 150 cm. British Museum, London, UK. Photo © The Trustees of the British Museum

p. 74   *Pericles's Funeral Oration*. Print, later colouring, after the painting, 1853, by Philipp von Foltz. Photo akg-images

p. 76   The Ancient Theatre of Epidaurus, Peloponnese, Greece. Photo © Stefanos Kyriazis / Dreamstime.com

p. 78   Caspar de Crayer, *Alexander and Diogenes*, c. 1625-1630. Oil on canvas, 196 × 278 cm. Photo © Rheinisches Bildarchiv Cologne (rba_c004455)

p. 80   Ruins of ancient Megalopolis with the cooling tower of a modern power station in the background, Megalopoli, Central Peloponnese, Greece. Photo Peter Eastland / Alamy Stock Photo

p. 82   Porta Maggiore, the remains of the aqueducts Aqua Claudia and Anio Novus (both 52 CE) integrated into the Aurelian Wall (271 CE), Rome, Italy. Photo © Dmitriy Moroz / Dreamstime.com

p. 84   Paved Roman Road across Blackstone Edge, Rishworth Moor, East of Littleborough, Greater Manchester, England. Photo Robert Estall Photo Agency / Alamy Stock Photo

p. 86   A Roman wall painting of Flora, goddess of flowers and spring. Fresco from the Villa di Arianna in Stabiae, near Pompeii, Italy, 1st century CE. National Archaeological Museum, Naples. Photo Nimatallah / akg-images

p. 88   Celsus Library, Ephesus, Turkey, 2nd century CE. Photo Images & Stories / Alamy Stock Photo

p. 90   Aedicula with small landscape, from the imperial villa at Boscotrecase, Naples, Campania, Italy. Early Imperial, Augustan, last decade of the 1st century BCE. Fresco on black ground, overall dimensions 233.1 × 114.3cm. Metropolitan Museum of Art, New York, Rogers Fund, 1920 (Acc. 20.192.1)

p. 92   Canaletto, *Ruins of the Forum looking towards the Capitol*, 1742. Oil on canvas, 190.0 × 106.2 cm. Royal Collection, London. Photo Royal Collection Trust / © His Majesty King Charles III, 2022 / Bridgeman Images

p. 96   Jean-Baptiste-Siméon Chardin, *The Scullery Maid*, c. 1738. Oil on canvas, 47 × 38.1 cm. National Gallery of Art, Washington, DC, USA, Corcoran Collection (William A. Clark Collection). Courtesy National Gallery of Art, Washington, DC

p. 98   Rembrandt van Rijn, *The Supper at Emmaus*, 1648. Oil on canvas, 68 × 65 cm. Musée du Louvre, Paris, France. Photo akg-images

p. 100   (left) Albrecht Dürer, *Adam*, 1507. Oil on wood, 209 × 81 cm. Prado, Madrid, Spain. Photo Erich Lessing / akg-images

p. 100   (right) Albrecht Dürer, *Eve*, 1507. Oil on wood, 209 × 80 cm. Prado, Madrid, Spain. Photo Erich Lessing / akg-images

p. 102   Gentile Bellini, *Procession of the True Cross (Procession of the brotherhood of San Giovanni Evangelista with the true cross relic on Saint Mark's day on the Piazza San Marco)*, 1496. Oil on canvas, 367 × 745 cm. Gallerie dell'Accademia, Venice, Italy. Photo Cameraphoto / akg-images

p. 104   Hubert and Jan van Eyck, *The Virgin Mary*, detail from the Ghent Altarpiece, 1423–1432. Saint-Bavo's Cathedral, Ghent, Belgium. Photo Hugo Maertens (www.artinflanders.be)

p. 106   Page from the *Codex Manesse*, Zürich, c. 1300–1340. Universitätsbibliothek Heidelberg. Photo Universitätsbibliothek Heidelberg / Cod. Pal. germ. 848 / p.178r

p. 108   Fra Angelico, *Noli Me Tangere*, c. 1442. Fresco photographed in situ at the Church and convent of San Marco, Florence, Italy. Photo © Scala, Florence

p. 110   Anonymous architect, the façade of Strasbourg Cathedral ('Plan A1'), Strasbourg, France, 1260. Drawing, 86 × 59 cm. Musée de l'œuvre Notre Dame de Strasbourg, France (inv. No. 2). Photo Musées de Strasbourg

p. 114   An eight-spoked wheel decorating the Hindu Konark Sun Temple in India, 13th century CE. Photo bajjibala / 123RF.com

p. 116   Fazal Sheikh, *Dawn Along the Yamuna River, Vrindavan, India*, 2003. From the 'Moksha' series. © Fazal Sheikh

p. 118   *Three aspects of the Absolute*, page 1 from a manuscript of the *Nath Charit* (attributed to Bulaki), 1823. Opaque watercolor, gold, and tin alloy on paper, 47 × 123 cm. Mehrangarh Museum, Jodhpur, Rajasthan, India. Photo courtesy Mehrangarh Museum Trust, Jodhpur, Rajasthan, India and His Highness Maharaja Gaj Singh of Jodhpur

p. 120   Ravi Varma Press, *Lakshmi*, 1894. Lithograph, 71.4 × 50.8 cm. Metropolitan Museum of Art, New York, USA, Purchase, Gift of Mrs. William J. Calhoun and Bequest of Nina Bunshaft, by exchange, 2013 (Acc. 2013.10)

p. 122   Yashoda with the Infant Krishna, Chola period, early 12th century. Copper alloy, 44.5 × 30 × 27.6 cm. Metropolitan Museum of Art, New York, USA, Purchase, Lita Annenberg Hazen Charitable Trust Gift, in honor of Cynthia Hazen and Leon B. Polsky, 1982 (Acc. 1982.220.8)

p. 124   Loving Couple (Mithuna), Orissa, India, Eastern Ganga dynasty, 13th century. Ferruginous stone, height 182.9 cm. Metropolitan Museum of Art, New York, USA. Purchase, Florance Waterbury Bequest, 1970 (Acc. 1970.44)

p. 128   Taidō Shūfū, *Ensō*, 19th century. Hanging scroll; ink on paper, 28.1 × 61.8 cm.

Minneapolis Institute of Arts, MN, USA. Photo © Minneapolis Institute of Art / Gift of the Friends of the Institute's Teahouse Fund / Bridgeman Images

p. 130   Sengai Gibon, Copy of *The Universe*. Hanging scroll; ink on paper, 110.5 × 56 cm. Arthur M. Sackler Gallery, Smithsonian Institution, Washington, DC: The Dr. Paul Singer Collection of Chinese Art of the Arthur M. Sackler Gallery, Smithsonian Institution; a joint gift of the Arthur M. Sackler Foundation, Paul Singer, the AMS Foundation for the Arts, Sciences, and Humanities, and the Children of Arthur M. Sackler (S2012.9.4606)

p. 132   Sesson Yūbai, *Poem on the Theme of a Monk's Life*, first half of the 14th century. Hanging scroll; ink on paper, 40.6 × 59.4 cm. Metropolitan Museum of Art, New York, USA, Gift of Sylvan Barnet and William Burto, in honour of Miyeko Murase, 2014 (Acc. 2014.719.7)

p. 134   Muqi Fachang, *Six Persimmons*, China, Southern Song dynasty, 13th century. Makota Sakurai / Alamy Stock Photo

p. 136   Figure of Budai Hesheng decorated in polychrome enamels and with biscuit-fired areas, by Liu Zhen (according to inscription), China, Ming Dynasty, 1486. Stoneware, 119.2 × 65 × 41 cm. British Museum, London, UK. Photo © The Trustees of the British Museum

p. 138   Dong Qichang, *Invitation to Reclusion at Jingxi*, China, Ming Dynasty, 1611. Handscroll, ink on paper, 26 × 92.6 cm. Metropolitan Museum of Art, New York, USA, Gift of Mr. and Mrs. Wan-go H. C. Weng, 1990 (Acc. 1990.318)

p. 140   Gardens of Tokai-an, Kyoto, Japan, 18th century. Photo © Ian Korn

p. 144   Ceiling of the Hall of the Ambassadors, Alcázar, Seville, Spain, 1427. Photo © Peter Bardwell

p. 146   Medallion carpet known as 'The Ardabil Carpet', Safavid Iran, dated 946H, 1539-1540. Wool knotted pile on silk foundation, c. 530 × 1032 cm. Victoria and Albert Museum, London, UK. Photo © Victoria and Albert Museum, London

p. 148   The garden of Ganjali Khan Caravanserai, Kerman, Iran. Photo © Evgeniy Fesenko / Dreamstime.com

p. 150   Patio de Arrayanes, The Comares Palace, the Alhambra, Granada, Spain. Photo © Ivan Soto / Dreamstime.com

p. 154   Fra Filippo Lippi, *Madonna and Child with Two Angels*, c. 1460-1465. Tempera on wood, 92 × 63 cm. Galleria degli Uffizi, Florence, Italy. Photo Rabatti & Domingie / akg-images

p. 156   Ca' d' Oro ("Golden House", Palazzo Santa Sofia), Grand Canal, Sestiere di Cannaregio, Venice, Italy. Photo © Demerzel21 / Dreamstime.com

p. 158   Galileo Galilei, *Six depictions of the moon*, 1609. Ink and pen on paper, Biblioteca Nazionale, Florence, Italy. Photo Rabatti & Domingie / akg-images

p. 160   Jean-Baptiste-Siméon Chardin, *The Governess*, c. 1739. Oil on canvas, 72.5 × 65 cm. Tatton Park, Cheshire. Photo The Egerton Collection / National Trust Photographic Library / John Hammond / Bridgeman Images

p. 162   Maurice Quentin de La Tour, *Portrait of la marquise de Pompadour* ('Madame Pompadour'), 1752-1755. Pastel on paper, 175 × 128 cm. Musée du Louvre, Paris, France. Photo Erich Lessing / akg-images

p. 164   Thomas Rowlandson, *The Successful Fortune Hunter, or Captain Shelalee Leading Miss Marrowfat to the Temple of Hymen*, 1802. Hand-coloured etching, 34.3 × 24.5 cm. Metropolitan Museum of Art, New York, USA, The Elisha Whittelsey Collection, The Elisha Whittelsey Fund, 1956 (Acc. 56.567.16)

p. 166   Quirijn van Brekelenkam, *Sentimental Conversation*, early 1660s. Oil on wood, 41.3 × 35.2 cm. Metropolitan Museum of Art, New York, USA, The Friedsam Collection, Bequest of Michael Friedsam, 1931 (Acc. 32.100.19)

p. 168   François Xavier Vispré, *Portrait of a Man Reclining on a Sofa, Reading*, 1750. Pastel drawing on vellum, 44.8 × 60.5 cm. Ashmolean Museum, Oxford, UK. Photo © Ashmolean Museum / Bridgeman Images

p. 172   'Their manner of fishynge in Virginia.' Engraving by Theodor de Bry after a watercolour painting by John White. From *A Briefe and True Report of the New Found Land of Virginia* written by Thomas Hariot (Frankfurt, 1590). John Carter Brown Library, Box 1894, Brown University, Providence, R.I. 02912

p. 174   Spiridione Roma, *The East Offering its Riches to Britannia*, 1778. Allegorical ceiling piece commissioned by the East India Company in 1777 for the Committee Room in East India House, London. Photo © British Library Board. All Rights Reserved / Bridgeman Images

p. 176   Engraving by Theodor de Bry, from *A Short Account of the Destruction of the Indies*, written by Bartolomé de las Casas (Frankfurt, 1598). Jay I. Kislak Collection, Rare Book and Special Collections Division, Library of Congress, Washington, DC

p. 178   Jean-Michel Moreau, 'C'est a ce prix que vous mangez du sucre en Europe' ('It is at this price that you eat sugar in Europe'), from an illustrated edition of Voltaire's *Candide*, 1787

p. 180   Joshua Reynolds, *Portrait of Syacust Ukah*, 1762. Oil on canvas, 120 × 89.9 cm. Gilcrease Museum, Tulsa, OK

p. 182   *Chief Charlo* [sic]. Photo of Chief Charlo, taken c. 1907. Library of Congress Prints and Photographs Division, Washington, DC (LC-USZ62-116119)

p. 186   Bill Brandt, *Northumberland Miner at his Evening Meal*, 1937. Bill Brandt © Bill Brandt Archive

p. 188   Timothy H. O'Sullivan, *A Harvest of Death, Gettysburg, Pennsylvania, July 4, 1863*, 1863. Albumen silver print by Alexander Gardner, 17.8 × 22.1 cm. The J. Paul Getty Museum, Los Angeles, CA (84.XO.1232.1.36 T)

p. 190   Philip James de Loutherbourg, *An Avalanche in the Alps*, 1803. Oil on canvas, 109 × 160 cm. Tate, London. Photo © Tate

p. 192   Positivist Temple to the Religion of Humanity, Porto Alegre, Brazil, late 19th century. Photo © Ricardo Calovi

p. 194   The Baptistery, Florence, Italy. Photo taken c. 1890–1900. Library of Congress Prints and Photographs Division, Washington, DC (LC-DIG-ppmsc-06457)

p. 198   Painting of a Hippopotamus, New Kingdom, Dynasty 18, c. 1479–1425 BCE, Metropolitan Museum of Art, New York, USA, Rogers Fund, 192 (Acc. 23.3.6)

p. 200   Tapper (iroke Ifa), Yoruba, Owo region, Nigeria, 17th or 18th century. Ivory, height 47 cm. Art Institute of Chicago, IL, Gift of Richard Faletti, the Faletti Family Collection

p. 202   Detail from a mosaic of a caravan and hunting scene, Bosra theatre, Hauran, Syria. Photo agefotostock / Alamy Stock Photo

p. 204   The Berlin conference, 1884. Wood engraving after a drawing by Adalbert von Rößler, from a late 19th century edition of 'Illustrierte Zeitung'

p. 206   Kenneth Scott Associates, Dr Easmon Residence, Accra, Ghana, 1959. Photo taken by J. J. Rose-Innes, 1959. RIBA Collections

p. 208   Stuart Franklin, *Lobby of the Gaweye Hotel, Niamey, Niger*. Picture taken 2005. © Stuart Franklin / Magnum Photos

p. 212   Walker Evans, *Subway Portrait*, New York, 1938. Gelatin silver print, 12.2 × 15 cm. Metropolitan Museum of Art, New York, USA. Inscribed: incomplete record. Gift of Arnold H. Crane, 1971 (Acc. 1971.646.18). Image © The Metropolitan Museum of Art / Art Resource / Scala, Florence

p. 214   Henri de Toulouse-Lautrec, *Au lit: le baiser*, 1892. Private Collection. Photo courtesy Sotheby's

p. 216   Edward Burtynsky, *Oil Refineries #23 (Oakville, Ontario), Canada*, 1999. Photo © Edward Burtynsky, courtesy Nicholas Metivier Gallery, Toronto

p. 218   Martin Parr, *Benidorm, Spain*, 2014. © Martin Parr / Magnum Photos

p. 220   A girl with electrodes on her head to record psychophysiological signals for

research purposes. Electrocardiogram (ECG),
electroencephalogram (EEG) and electrooculogram
(EOG) being recorded. Photo Latsalomao / iStock

p. 222   Hubble Ultra Deep Field, composited
from data gathered from images captured by
the Advanced Camera for Surveys during 400
Hubble orbits around Earth, and taken between
24th September 2003 and 16th January 2004.
Photo NASA, ESA, S. Beckwith (STScI) and the
HUDF Team

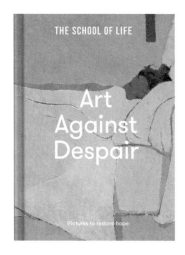

Art Against Despair

Pictures to restore hope

An inspiring selection of images offering us hope and comfort, reminding us that we are not alone in our sorrow.

One of the most unexpectedly useful things we can do when we're feeling glum or out of sorts is to look at pictures. The best works of art can lift our spirits, remind us of what we love and return perspective to our situation. A few moments in front of the right picture can rescue us.

This is a collection of the world's most consoling and uplifting images, accompanied by small essays that talk about the works in a way that offers us comfort and inspiration. The images in the book range wildly across time and space: from ancient to modern art, east to west, north to south, taking in photography, painting, abstract and figurative art. All the images have been carefully chosen to help us with a particular problem we might face: a broken heart, a difficulty at work, the meanness of others, the challenges of family and friends ...

We're invited to look at art with unusual depth and then find our way towards new hope and courage. This is a portable museum dedicated to beauty and consolation, a unique book about art which is also about psychology and healing: a true piece of art therapy.

ISBN: 978-1-912891-90-0
£22.00 | $32.99

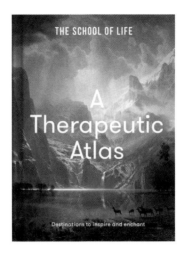

A Therapeutic Atlas

Destinations to inspire and enchant

A selection of unique and beautiful destinations around the world, which offer powerful new perspectives on life.

The world is full of places with an unusual power to inspire and bring us joy; they might be exceptionally beautiful, resonant with history, untouched by civilization or rich in the right sort of memories.

This is an atlas that gathers together some of the most enchanting and reinvigorating places around the world in order to heal and captivate us. A perfect book for keen travellers, it takes us to beautiful destinations in Greece, Italy, Japan, America, Chile and Australia – to name but a few. We're taken to the tops of mountains, to solitary cliffs, elegant cities – and also to some less expected locations: airports, hydroelectric stations and meteorite craters.

Great travellers have always known that travelling can broaden the mind; here we see how it can also heal it. Tempting images are combined with short essays that discuss the power of particular places to help us with the difficulties of being human. We visit places that are 'therapeutic' because they coax us out of familiar patterns of thought and liberate our minds.

This is a book that can be read when we are travelling or when we are at home, it will remind us of the many places we still want to see – and more broadly, the many reasons we have to stay hopeful.

ISBN: 978-1-912891-93-1
£22.00 | $32.99